Czech & Slovak Kolaches & Sweet T

Collected by

The Museum Guild of the National Czech & Slovak Museum

Associate editors: Miriam Canter, Melinda Bradnan, Dorothy Crum, Ju
Dwayne Bourret, and Joan Liffring-Zug Bourret
Graphic design: Deborah Walkoczy and Ericka Robinson

Front cover: Wild red poppies in the Czech Republic, Joan Liffring-Zug
Illustrations by Diane Heusinkveld

Penfield
Press

Acknowledgments

Thanks to all the members of the Museum Guild of the National Czech & Slovak Museum & Library, Cedar Rapids, Iowa. Special thanks to Shirley Rosencrans of the Museum Store and to Guild members Fern Fackler and Sylvia Rohlena for their guidance. We especially thank, also, Toni Birmingham and other members of the Phillips (Wisconsin) Czechoslovakian Community Festival Committee for their group's wonderful contribution to this collection, and Betty Hosticka of Sokol Greater Cleveland for arranging permission to reprint recipes from their centennial cookbook. And to all contributors, friends of the Guild and Penfield Press, who are listed with their recipes, we thank you for your continued interest in bringing these mini-pleasures-of-cooking to fruition.

ISBN 1-57216-093-4
©Penfield Press 2001
www.penfieldbooks.com

"Kolache" Memories
by Juanita Loven

How should you spell ko-la-che? *Kolac* or *kolace* or *kolache* or *kolacky?* No matter how it is spelled, this fruit-filled bread is delicious!

The origin of the kolache is uncertain. One version goes like this: "A mother, busy with her weekly baking, broke off a few pieces of dough to keep her little daughter occupied. The little cook kneaded her dough into flat cakes. She selected several plums from a bowl on the table and placed the fruit in the center of the round piece of dough. Her cake went into the oven along with Mother's bread. The father, coming in from a long day in the fields, picked up the cake cooling on the table and took a bite. The hot juice of the plum spurted into his mouth, causing him to hop

around on one foot in a circle around the table. The little girl shouted with glee saying, '*Tatinek* (father) ... *kolac.*' And that is how the kolache got its name. Soon the fame of the kolache spread throughout the Czech-Austro-Hungarian empire and on to the New World." (*Fraternal Herald W.F.L.A.*, January, 1980)

My kolache memories begin with my mother's Czech/German version. She used either a sweet roll recipe or extra bread dough for her "open-faced" version. Her usual fillings were prune, apple, cherry, or sweetened, sieved cottage cheese. She usually sprinkled them with streusel (a mixture of flour, vanilla, sugar, and butter) before baking.

I had never seen a "closed" kolache until we moved to Spillville, Iowa. The closed version takes a little more shaping: Put a rounded tablespoon of filling on a square of flattened dough, pulling and pinching two opposite corners together, following the same procedure with the other two corners before the final raising. This method allows

a peek at the filling and makes them more stackable. The Spillville Czech ladies filled their kolaches with prune, poppy seed, apricot, cherry, or apple filling; each had their favorite dough recipe. The open-faced and closed versions are heavenly.

TIME-TESTED TIPS

In the Czech Republic kolaches are often served in a round pan rather than individually. To make: Prepare dough as usual. After letting dough rise in a bowl, divide into two or more large rounds. Place each round into two or more 10-inch-round, greased baking pans. Press down centers to form a raised edge around the outside. Spread filling of your choice over the top as artistically as you wish. For example, you could place prune filling in the center, then a strip of cottage cheese filling, followed by a strip of apricot filling, completing the work of art by adding nuts, raisins, streusel, etc. Brush the dough edges with egg white and bake in a preheated 325° oven for 30 minutes.

HOW TO SHAPE KOLACHES

Closed: Roll or pat out dough to about 1/2- to 3/4-inch thickness. Cut in strips about 3 inches wide. Cut again into squares. Stretch out corners of each square. Put filling of choice in center of each. Take up two opposite corners and pinch together; repeat. Let rise and bake. This method is stackable and allows a peek at the filling.

Open-faced: Prepare as above but form individual balls. Flatten and let rise a little in greased baking pan (twelve to a 9 x 13" pan). Using thumbs or fingers, press down center of each and place a tablespoon of filling in each. Let rise again and bake. Take care to flatten center before filling; this keeps filling from running over while baking.

For the Love of Kolaches
by Pat Martin

Living in a Czech community, we become accustomed to visitors seeking kolaches to purchase. I have witnessed enjoyment of kolaches as "centerpiece desserts" at many special comunity events heralding the fact that Cedar Rapids is a Czech capital of sorts. Although these goodies are a spectacular treat to the uninitiated, within the Czech communities, the kolache is a staple! In Czech and Slovak homes, kolaches are served frequently. There is a joke that there are six, not five, basic food groups in the Czech diet—kolaches being the sixth.

I've observed that "foreigners" to the kolache select the cherry or peach varieties, while kolache purists, generally Czechs or Slovaks themselves, prefer the poppy seed

or prune.

Another observation is that many of us modern women struggle with a pie crust made from scratch two or three times a year, but Czech and Slovak cooks are undaunted baking dozens of kolaches on a Saturday morning! Whether served at breakfast, lunch, snack, or dinner once a lifetime, year, or week, the kolache is ambrosia.

Made for centuries as a soft pastry brush for basting kolaches, bread, and rolls, the Peroutka (feather baster) is still popular today. Goose feathers are washed, dried, stripped and then woven together with a cord. These can be purchased at the National Czech & Slovak Museum & Library Store.

For the Love of Poppy Seed
by Fern Kaplan Fackler

Poppy seeds may be harvested from four colors of poppies. A representative of the Czech Republic Embassy, Washington, D.C., says that red poppies are considered a weed in the Czech Republic, so they use the seed of only white poppies. The poppy seeds used in baking and for bird seed come from the common poppy: white, pink, red, or purple. The opium that is derived from poppies of all four colors comes from the young capsules processed prior to their developing the seeds.

The source of the Czech community's poppy seed during World War II was red poppies, planted abundantly between rows of green vegetable plants. Toward the end of the growing season, after the poppy petals fell and the plants began their drying

cycle, it would soon be time to gather the seeds.

I vividly recall with fondness the gathering season. A good "poppy seed gatherer" knew when to cut the dried stalks. We took the goose-roasting pan into the garden. My mother taught me to place the cut stalk with the seed pod carefully into the roaster so only a few of the tiny seeds would be lost. Later, we sat down to shake the pods and watched and listened as the poppy seeds fell from the row of holes encircling the pod just under the top. When the soft maraca-like sound stopped, we knew the seeds were out, and the baking could begin.

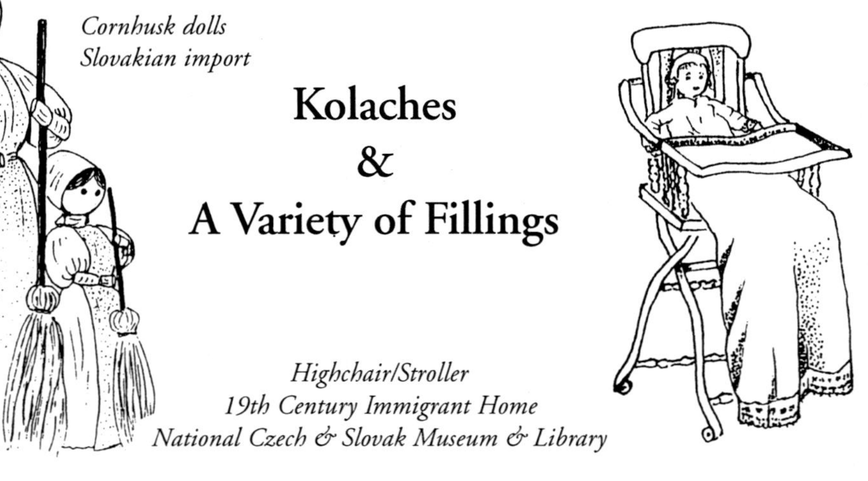

Kolaches
&
A Variety of Fillings

No-Knead Refrigerator Kolache

This recipe, from The Best Czech Cooking and Collected Recipes of Helen Fiala, *is used for kolaches served at the Phillips (Wisconsin) Czechoslovakian Community Festival, held mid-June annually. As soon as school is out, the festival baking crew moves into the school kitchen, and the production of as many as 7,000 kolaches begins!*

4 cups flour
1/2 cup shortening
1/2 cup butter or margarine
1 teaspoon salt
1 package dry yeast
1/2 cup warm water
1/4 cup plus 1 teaspoon sugar, divided

1 cup cold milk
4 egg yolks
Streusel:
3 tablespoons flour
3 tablespoons sugar
2 tablespoons butter

Measure flour, shortening, butter, and salt into a bowl. Mix as for pie crust. Dissolve yeast in the warm water. Add 1 teaspoon sugar. Let rise until it bubbles. Put milk into a bowl and add remaining sugar and the egg yolks. Beat together, then add the yeast mixture to milk mixture. Pour liquid mixture into flour mixture, folding in until all flour is absorbed. Put dough on a floured board and knead into a ball. Put into a greased bowl, cover, and refrigerate overnight or at least 4 hours. When ready to bake, put dough on a floured board and shape into an oblong roll. Divide roll into four pieces and, again, shape each piece into an oblong roll. Cut each roll into thirteen pieces, roll into balls, and put on lightly greased baking pans. Cover and let rise until doubled. Prepare the streusel by mixing the flour, sugar, and butter until crumbly. Set aside. After rolls have risen, depress centers of each and fill with filling of your choice. Sprinkle with streusel and let rise again. Bake at 375° for 10 to 15 minutes.

continued

No-Knead Refrigerator Kolache continued

Note: Make a cloth depressor to press down centers. Cut a 7-inch square of cloth. Put 2 rounded tablespoons of flour in the center of cloth and twist ends together to make a tight ball. Secure tightly with string or a plastic bag twisty tie to make a compressed ball. Use for pressing down uniform centers. May be placed in a plastic bag and stored in freezer for reuse.

Bottle, handmade in the Czech Republic

Icebox Kolache

Vera Machovsky Hanson, Marion, Iowa

2 packages dry yeast
1/2 cup lukewarm coffee cream
2 tablespoons sugar
3/4 pound butter (no substitutes)
4 cups flour
6 egg yolks, beaten
1/4 teaspoon salt

1/2 teaspoon grated lemon rind
1 teaspoon vanilla
1 beaten egg for brushing and sealing
Crumb topping:
3/4 cup flour
1/3 cup margarine
1/2 cup sugar

Dissolve yeast in the lukewarm cream, add sugar, and set aside to rise. Using a pie crust blender, cut butter into flour to make fine crumbs. Add beaten egg yolks, the yeast

continued

Icebox Kolache continued

mixture, salt, lemon rind, and vanilla. Beat until dough is smooth. Cover and place in refrigerator overnight. The next day roll out dough on a pastry cloth to 1/4-inch thickness and cut into 2-inch squares. Spoon filling of choice onto center of each square. Brush corners with the beaten egg, bring together, and seal well. Prepare crumb topping by blending all ingredients together with a pie crust blender to make fine crumbs. Brush top with the beaten egg, sprinkle crumb topping over each, and place on ungreased baking sheet. Bake at 400° for 10 to 12 minutes.

Glass flower, handmade in the Czech Republic

Kolaches

Helen Horak Nemec

Helen Horak Nemec grew up near Czech Village in Cedar Rapids, Iowa, and worked at Sykora's Bakery in the village. This recipe makes six dozen kolaches.

2 packages dry yeast	2 whole eggs plus 4 yolks
1/4 cup lukewarm water	1/2 teaspoon mace
1/2 cup plus 1 tablespoon sugar, divided	1-1/2 teaspoons salt
1-1/4 cups butter or margarine, divided	1/2 teaspoon grated lemon rind
2 cups milk	6 to 7 cups flour

Dissolve yeast in lukewarm water; add 1 tablespoon of the sugar and let set until bubbly. Melt butter. Combine 1 cup butter and milk; heat until warm. Beat eggs and

continued

yolks, add sugar and beat until thickened. Add milk and butter mixture to the eggs, then add yeast mixture, mace, salt, and lemon rind. Beat in flour 1 cup at a time. When dough becomes too thick to beat with a wooden spoon, turn out on floured surface and knead until smooth and silky. Put into a greased bowl and let rise in a warm place until doubled. Turn dough out on lightly floured board, divide into six large pieces. Cut each of the large pieces into twelve smaller pieces. Form into walnut-size balls. Place on a greased baking sheet and brush each ball with melted butter. Let rise again until doubled in size. Press down center and fill with filling of choice. Let rise once more until light. Bake at 400° for 7 to 10 minutes. Brush with melted butter after removing from the oven.

Potato Kolache

Vera Machovsky Hanson, Marion, Iowa

2 packages dry yeast
1 cup lukewarm potato water, divided
1 cup plus 1 tablespoon sugar, divided
1 cup lukewarm milk
8 cups flour, divided
1/2 cup plus 1 tablespoon melted
    margarine, divided
2 teaspoons salt

2 teaspoons vanilla
1 teaspoon grated lemon rind
1 cup mashed potatoes
2 whole eggs plus 2 yolks, beaten
Crumb topping:
3/4 cup flour
1/3 cup margarine
1/2 cup sugar

Dissolve yeast in 1/4 cup of warm potato water, add 1 tablespoon sugar, and let rise until bubbly. Mix warm milk and remaining potato water; add 1 cup of flour and

continued

mix well. Add yeast mixture and set aside to rise as a "sponge." Add 1/2 cup melted margarine, remaining sugar, salt, vanilla, and lemon rind to the mashed potatoes. Mix well, then add beaten eggs and beat well. Mix in yeast mixture. Gradually add flour 1/2 cup at a time; beat well after each addition until the dough is not sticky. Cover and refrigerate overnight.

Next day, blend ingredients for crumb topping to make fine crumbs; set aside. Place chilled dough on a lightly floured pastry cloth. Work quickly to form into walnut-size balls and place about 1-1/2 inches apart on baking sheets that are greased or covered with parchment paper. Brush the balls with melted shortening; let rise until doubled. Make an indent in each and fill with choice of filling. Sprinkle with crumb topping. Let rise again, about 30 minutes. Bake in preheated 450° oven 12 to 15 minutes until lightly browned. Remove from oven and brush with melted margarine.

Refrigerator Dough for Kolaches or Rolls

Sylvia Rohlena, Cedar Rapids, Iowa

2 packages dry yeast
1/2 cup sugar
1 cup lukewarm water
2 sticks melted butter
3/4 cup milk
1 cup cold water
2 eggs
1 teaspoon salt
6 cups unsifted flour

In a large bowl, dissolve yeast and sugar in the warm water. Stir in melted butter and milk, then add cold water. Add eggs one at a time and mix thoroughly. Add salt and flour a little at a time, mixing until not sticky. Place dough in refrigerator for at least 2 hours or overnight. Form into desired shape. Let rise and bake in preheated 425° oven for 10 minutes.

Mom's Bread Machine Kolaches

Marilyn Tucker, Cedar Rapids, Iowa

1 tablespoon dry yeast
3-1/4 cups flour
1/3 cup plus 1 tablespoon powdered
   milk
1 teaspoon salt
3/8 cup sugar
1 egg

1/2 cup shortening, softened
1-1/8 cups warm water
Filling of choice
Streusel topping
Melted butter
Powdered sugar

Combine yeast, flour, powdered milk, salt, sugar, egg, shortening, and warm water in
bread machine container. After mixed, place dough in a large greased bowl; cover and

refrigerate at least 4 hours or overnight. Place dough on a generously floured board, and shape pieces of dough into walnut-size balls. Space balls 2 inches apart on greased baking sheet and let rise until doubled. Make an indent in center of each and fill with filling of choice. Let rise another 20 minutes until dough feels soft to the touch. Sprinkle topping on each kolache and bake at 375° for 10 minutes. Remove from oven and brush edges with melted butter. Remove to cooling racks and sift a little powdered sugar over each kolache.

Note: Add sugar and/or flavoring to taste to a prepared poppy seed or cherry pie filling. Dough may be kept refrigerated for baking a few kolaches or plain biscuits at a time.

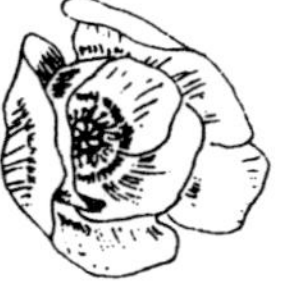

Old Czech Method Kolaches

Mana Machovsky Zlatohlavek, Cedar Rapids, Iowa

6 cups flour

1/2 cup plus 1 teaspoon sugar, divided

1-1/2 cups warm milk, divided

2 packages active dry yeast

1-1/2 teaspoons salt

3/4 cup butter or margarine, melted

1 egg plus 2 yolks or 2 whole eggs,
    well beaten

2 teaspoons vanilla

1 teaspoon grated lemon rind or extract

Crumb topping:

3/4 cup flour

1/3 cup butter

1/2 cup sugar

Sift flour into large bowl. Make a well in the flour. Put 1 teaspoon sugar, 1/2 cup of the warm milk, and yeast in the well. Let stand about 5 minutes. Add remaining

sugar, the salt, shortening, eggs, 3/4 cup of the milk (remaining 1/4 cup to use as necessary), vanilla, and lemon rind. Mix and beat well with a wooden spoon. Sprinkle top lightly with flour, cover, and let rise in a warm place about 1-1/2 hours. Then turn onto floured board, divide, and shape into three long rolls. Cut off pieces about the size of a large walnut and form into balls. Place on a greased pan or baking sheet about 1-1/2 inches apart and brush with melted butter or margarine. Let rise again until doubled in size. Prepare crumb topping: Blend all ingredients to make fine crumbs. Press down centers of each roll and fill with filling of choice. (Solo brand fillings are good to use.) Sprinkle with the crumb topping if desired and let rise again for 15 to 20 minutes. Bake in 425° preheated oven for 12 to 15 minutes. Remove from oven and brush with melted shortening. Makes 5-1/2 to 6 dozen.

Kolache

Helen E. Fritz

From the Wilber Czech Museum, Wilber, Nebraska. Submitted by Lillian Wanek.

2 cakes fresh yeast

1/4 cup lukewarm water

2 cups scalded milk

3/4 cup sugar

2/3 cup melted butter

2 eggs

6 cups flour

2 teaspoons salt

In a large mixing bowl, dissolve yeast in the warm water. Add remaining ingredients and beat well. Shape into small balls and place on a greased baking pan about 1 inch apart. Let rise until light. Press down centers and fill with desired fillings. Let rise again and bake at 350° for 12 to 15 minutes.

Kolache Dough

Lydia Elias, Cedar Rapids, Iowa

3 packages yeast (or 6-3/4 teaspoons)

3-3/4 cups milk including 1 (12-ounce) can evaporated milk, lukewarm

2/3 cup sugar

3 teaspoons salt

1/4 cup potato flakes or 1 cup mashed potatoes (optional for moist dough)

8 cups flour, divided

6 egg yolks

1/2 cup margarine melted together with 1/2 cup Crisco or lard or 3/4 cup vegetable oil

1/2 cup melted shortening or margarine to brush

In a large bowl, dissolve yeast in lukewarm milk to which sugar and salt have been added. If desired, add potato to yeast mixture. Mix in about 5 cups of the flour. Beat

continued

in egg yolks, beat well with mixer, and let stand until spongy. Then add the combined shortenings. Add remaining flour and mix with a wooden spoon. Sprinkle light layer of flour over dough, cover with plastic wrap or waxed paper, and let rise in a warm place until doubled. Place dough on a floured board and form pieces into walnut-size balls. Put balls on a greased baking sheet, at least 1 inch apart. Brush with melted shortening and let rise again until doubled, 20 to 25 minutes. Press indentation into each ball and fill with favorite fillings. Let rise again for about 5 to 10 minutes. Bake at 375° about 10 to 12 minutes. Start on lower shelf of oven and move to top shelf after about 5 minutes. Watch rolls closely the last few minutes to make sure bottoms do not burn. Remove from oven and brush with melted butter or margarine. Transfer to paper towels and cover with a tea towel to retain moisture during cooling.

Old-Style Kolaches

Ed Nejdl, Cedar Rapids, Iowa

Mrs. Steve Slepicka submitted a similar recipe, which suggests using either chicken fat, duck fat, or pork lard.

2 cups milk, scalded
2/3 cup sugar
2 packages dry yeast
1-1/2 teaspoons salt
1 whole egg

2 egg yolks
1/3 cup butter
1/3 cup chicken fat (if not available, use butter)
6 cups flour, divided

Scald milk; add sugar and cool to lukewarm. Add yeast to lukewarm mixture and let rise. Stir in remaining ingredients, using only half of the flour until mixed evenly,

continued

Old-Style Kolaches continued

then add remaining flour. Mix thoroughly with wooden spoon or mixer bread hook. Store in refrigerator overnight. When ready to bake, shape dough into small, walnut-size balls. Grease the balls; place on greased baking sheet and let rise until doubled in size. Press center of each ball with your thumb. Fill indentation with filling of choice and let rise again until light. Bake in preheated 425° oven for 12 minutes. When done, brush tops with melted butter. Makes about 5 dozen.

Blown-glass fruit ornaments were hung on trees as symbolic gifts, when fruit was unobtainable in Central Europe at Christmastime. Even today, fruit is a symbolic gift on St. Nicholas Day, December 6.
　　　—In the collection of the museum store of the National Czech & Slovak
　　　　Museum & Library

Ice Cream Kolache

4 cups flour
2 tablespoons sugar
1 pound butter

1 pint vanilla ice cream, softened
Apricot, prune, or cheese filling

Combine flour and sugar in a mixing bowl. Cut in butter until mixture resembles cornmeal. Add softened ice cream and mix thoroughly. Wrap in foil and chill for several hours or overnight. Roll out 1/4 inch thick on a lightly floured surface. Using a knife or pastry wheel, cut into squares or rounds. Make a slight depression in the center of each and fill with suggested fillings or preserves. Bake at 350° for 20 to 25 minutes until lightly browned.

Kolache Dainties

Vilma Nejdl, Ely, Iowa

2 packages yeast
1/2 cup half-and-half cream, lukewarm
2 tablespoons sugar
4 cups sifted flour
3/4 pound butter

6 egg yolks, beaten
1/4 teaspoon mace
1/4 teaspoon salt
1/2 teaspoon grated lemon rind
1 whole egg, beaten

Dissolve yeast in lukewarm cream, add sugar, and set aside to rise. Measure flour into a bowl and cut in butter until mixture is crumbly. Add beaten egg yolks, mace, salt, and rind to yeast mixture, then add this mixture to flour mixture and beat until dough is stiff and smooth. Cover and place in refrigerator overnight. The next day,

roll out dough 1/4 inch thick and cut into small squares, approximately 2 inches square. Place your choice of filling in center of each square, brush each corner with beaten egg, bring corners together, and seal. Brush tops of each with beaten egg and place on ungreased baking sheet. Bake at 400° for 10 to 12 minutes until lightly browned. Yields 6-1/2 to 7 dozen.

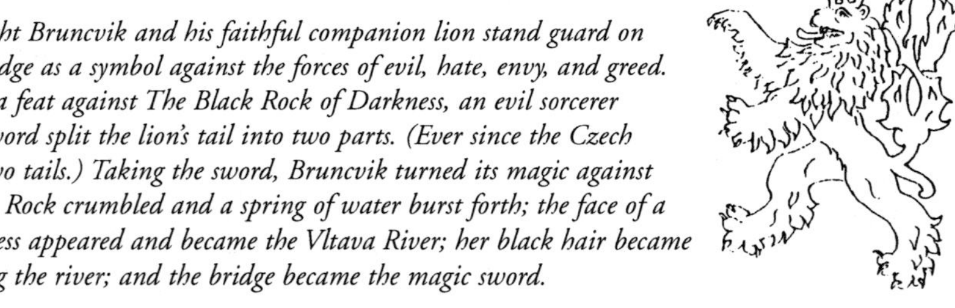

The brave knight Bruncvik and his faithful companion lion stand guard on the Charles Bridge as a symbol against the forces of evil, hate, envy, and greed. Legend tells of a feat against The Black Rock of Darkness, an evil sorcerer whose magic sword split the lion's tail into two parts. (Ever since the Czech lion has had two tails.) Taking the sword, Bruncvik turned its magic against evil; The Black Rock crumbled and a spring of water burst forth; the face of a beautiful princess appeared and became the Vltava River; her black hair became the houses along the river; and the bridge became the magic sword.

Mock Cherry Kolaches

1 cup butter
1-1/2 cups sugar
4 eggs
2-1/2 cups flour

1 teaspoon baking powder
1 teaspoon vanilla
1 teaspoon almond extract
1 to 2 cans cherry pie filling

Cream butter and sugar together. Add eggs and beat well. Stir in flour, baking powder, vanilla, and almond extract to form a thick batter. Spread batter into a greased 10 x 15-inch baking pan. With a knife, score batter into 24 squares. Spoon about 1 tablespoon of filling into center of each square. Bake at 350° for 30 to 40 minutes. When done, cut into 24 squares. Sprinkle with powdered sugar if desired.

Cake-Mix Kolaches

2 packages dry yeast	5 cups flour
2-1/2 cups warm water, divided	2 eggs
1 package yellow cake mix	Desired filling

Soften yeast in 1/2 cup of the warm water. Mix cake mix, flour, remaining water, and eggs. Add yeast mixture and mix to make a soft dough (add more flour if needed). Place dough in a greased bowl, cover, and let rise until doubled. Punch down and shape pieces of dough into large walnut-size balls. Place on a greased baking sheet and let rise again. Indent center of each and fill with 1 tablespoon of desired filling. Let rise until doubled. Bake at 375° for 15 to 20 minutes.

Babi's Cottage Cheese Kolaches

Cathy Cropp-Scanlon, Cedar Rapids, Iowa

Cathy re-creates Grandmother Mabel Mundil Votroubek's recipe for no yeast kolaches, noting that she stirred by hand and baked them in a wood-stove oven.

2 cups cottage cheese, divided (add a
    little sugar if you use low-fat)
1 cup butter (no substitutes)
2 eggs, separated
2 cups flour
1 teaspoon baking powder
1/2 teaspoon salt

Cottage cheese filling:
2 egg whites
1/4 cup sugar
1 teaspoon cinnamon
1/2 teaspoon nutmeg
Raisins
Remaining cottage cheese

Beat cottage cheese until smooth. Measure out 1 cup and set aside for filling. Add butter to remaining cottage cheese and blend well. Add two egg yolks and beat well. Mix dry ingredients together and add slowly to the egg/cheese mixture. Add flour as needed to make a non-sticky dough. Take pieces (about 2 tablespoons) of dough and roll into a ball. Place ball on a greased baking sheet and make a deep depression in the center. Prepare filling: Beat egg whites until foamy, stir in dry ingredients, and add remaining cottage cheese. If you like, put a few raisins in each kolache and fill with the cottage cheese filling or other filling of choice. Do not overfill since it will bubble over and burn. Bake in 350° oven for 15 to 20 minutes. Just before serving, sprinkle with powdered sugar if desired. Makes about 1-1/2 dozen.

Sour Cream Kolacky

Sokol Greater Cleveland Cookbook, Centennial 1997 Issue

A similar recipe was submitted by Marie Kluck, Palos Park, Illinois.

1 small cake compressed yeast
1/4 cup warm water (not too hot)
5 cups all-purpose flour
1/2 cup sugar
1 teaspoon salt
1 teaspoon baking powder
1 pound butter or margarine
4 egg yolks
1/2 pint sour cream (or imitation)
2 teaspoons vanilla

1 egg, beaten with several drops of water
    for egg wash topping
Prepared fruit filling (apricot, prune,
    poppy seed, or nut)
Walnuts or coconut, finely chopped
Crumb mixture: (optional)
2 tablespoons margarine
3 tablespoons sugar
4 tablespoons flour

Heat oven to 375°. Dissolve yeast in warm water; stir to mix. Combine dry ingredients. Add butter or margarine and cut in until mixture is crumbly and pea size. Add egg yolks, sour cream, and vanilla to yeast mixture; mix well and add to flour mixture. Mix well and place dough in refrigerator for a few hours or overnight. To shape: Place dough on lightly floured cloth or board and roll out to 1/8-inch thickness. Cut into 2- to 2-1/2-inch circles or squares. Brush each with egg wash; top with a teaspoon of filling of choice, depressing slightly into dough. Crumb mixture: Mix and rub together all ingredients until crumbly. Sprinkle filled kolacky with chopped nuts, coconut, or crumb mixture. Bake in preheated oven for 10 to 12 minutes, until golden brown. Cool on a rack.

Note: Dough may be wrapped in plastic and frozen for several weeks. Thaw to room temperature before rolling out.

Nutty Pocketbooks

Fern Kaplan Fackler, Cedar Rapids, Iowa
Fern submits this recipe in loving memory of her mother, Leona Netolicky Kaplan.

Favorite kolache dough
Nut filling:
3 tablespoons butter
3 cups ground nuts, divided

Pinch of salt
1/2 cup sugar
1/2 teaspoon vanilla
Melted butter for brushing

Using your favorite kolache dough, roll into balls somewhat larger than for regular kolaches. Flatten to 1/4 inch thick. Prepare the filling: Melt butter in a saucepan; add 2-1/4 cups of the nuts (reserve remaining for topping). Add salt, sugar, and vanilla. Stir well for about 5 minutes. If it is too thick, add a little milk, just so the

mixture is firm and will not run. Place a tablespoon of filling in the center of flattened rounds. Fold over to form a half circle. Press dough around edge to seal. Put pockets, seal side down, on greased baking sheet. Brush with melted butter. Let rise for about a half hour. Bake in a 425° oven for 10 to 12 minutes or until lightly browned. Remove from pan to cool. Brush with melted butter. To serve, frost with a white frosting and dip into reserved ground nuts. Makes 3-1/2 to 4 dozen.

Blown-glass swan ornament, symbol of gratefulness

A Variety of Fillings and Toppings for Kolaches

Cabbage Filling

1 small head of cabbage, shredded

1 teaspoon sugar

Salt and pepper

1 tablespoon butter

Spread cabbage in a jelly roll pan. Sprinkle lightly with sugar, and the salt and pepper. Dot with butter and bake at 350° until tender and starts to brown. Put a heaping teaspoonful of filling in the center of each kolache, seal, and let rise.

Farmer's Cheese Filling

3 (7-1/2 ounce) bars farmer's cheese

1/2 cup sugar

1-1/2 teaspoons grated lemon rind

1/2 cup raisins

Mix all ingredients together and spoon into center of each kolache.

Prune Filling

2 pounds cooked pitted prunes

12 gingersnaps

1 cup brown sugar

Cinnamon and salt to taste

Drain prunes; grind gingersnaps and prunes together. Add remaining ingredients and mix. Use for open or closed kolaches.

Apricot or Prune Filling

3 cups dried apricots or prunes

1/4 cup sugar

1/2 teaspoon cinnamon

Stew apricots or prunes. If using prunes, pit after cooking. Cool. Run through a food grinder, then add sugar and cinnamon. Fill indentations in kolaches with tablespoonfuls of mixture.

Apricot Filling

1 pound dried apricots

Sugar to taste

Finely ground almonds to taste

Cook apricots until tender. Grind and mix with the sugar and almonds. Use for open or closed kolaches.

Cottage Cheese Filling

1 pound cottage cheese, dry or drained

1 (8-ounce) package cream cheese

2 egg yolks

2 teaspoons vanilla

3/4 cup sugar

3 tablespoons flour

1/2 teaspoon cinnamon

Cream cheeses. Mix remaining ingredients and add to creamed cheeses.

Pineapple Filling

Norma Newmeister, Cedar Rapids, Iowa

1 (13-1/2 ounce) can sweetened,
   crushed pineapple
1/4 cup water
1/4 cup sugar
2 tablespoons cornstarch
2 tablespoons butter

Cook pineapple, water, sugar, and cornstarch until thick. Stir in butter. Cool before using.

Pineapple Filling with Egg

Lydia Elias, Cedar Rapids, Iowa

1-2/3 cups crushed pineapple
1 tablespoon lemon juice
2 tablespoons cornstarch
1 egg, beaten
1 tablespoon butter
1/4 teaspoon salt

Cook together until thick. Cool before using.

Glass fruit, hand-made in the Czech Republic

Cottage Cheese Filling with Egg

Norma Newmeister, Cedar Rapids, Iowa

1-1/2 cups cottage cheese, drained
1/4 cup sugar
1 tablespoon lemon juice

1 egg, beaten
1/4 cup chopped nuts
Maraschino cherries, halved

Mix first five ingredients. Fill kolaches and place half a cherry on each.

Cream Cheese Filling

Lydia Elias, Cedar Rapids, Iowa

2 (8-ounce) packages cream cheese
2 eggs
1 teaspoon vanilla

3/4 cup sugar
Cherry pie filling

Mix all ingredients except cherry pie filling together well. Fill indentation of kolache. Add a big drop of cherry pie filling.

Poppy Seed Filling with Cream

2 cups finely ground poppy seed
1/2 cup cream
1/2 cup corn syrup

1 tablespoon butter
Cinnamon to taste

Mix together and cook in top of a double boiler until thick. Put a tablespoonful into each kolache.

Poppy Seed Filling

3 cups finely ground poppy seed
1 cup milk or more as needed

1/2 cup sugar or 1/3 cup honey

Place ground poppy seed in a saucepan. Add milk, sugar, or honey. Slowly bring to a boil. Cool before spooning into kolaches.

Poppy Seed Filling with Honey

Lydia Elias, Cedar Rapids, Iowa

1 can prepared poppy seed filling

1-1/2 to 2 cups raisins

3/4 can of milk (use filling can)

1 tablespoon honey

1 tablespoon sugar

1 teaspoon vanilla extract

1/4 teaspoon almond extract

Graham cracker crumbs, enough to thicken mixture

1/4 cup chopped pecans (optional)

Mix all ingredients together. May be used uncooked or cook to almost boiling.

Crumb Topping for Kolaches

1 cup flour

1/2 cup sugar

1/4 cup butter or margarine

1/4 teaspoon salt (omit if using margarine)

1/4 teaspoon cinnamon

Using a pastry blender, mix all ingredients together until crumbly.

Sweetened Butter Topping

Lydia Elias, Cedar Rapids, Iowa

1 cup flour

1 cup sugar

1/4 cup butter

Mix all ingredients until crumbly. Sprinkle over kolache filling to keep filling from overflowing during baking.

Cherry Filling

1 cup sugar

6 tablespoons cornstarch

1/4 teaspoon salt

2 cans red sour cherries

1 teaspoon red food coloring

1 teaspoon vanilla

1/2 teaspoon almond flavoring

Mix sugar, cornstarch, and salt. Add juice from cherries. Cook and stir until thick. Add remaining ingredients. Makes enough to fill 3 dozen kolaches.

Butter-Nut Topping
Beatrice Kriz Lala, submitted by Marge Lala Stone, Cedar Rapids, Iowa

3 teaspoons butter or margarine

Nutmeg to taste

Enough sugar to make good and sweet

Chopped nuts

Enough flour to make crumbly

Cream together butter and sugar; cut in flour. Stir in nutmeg and nuts.

Sausage Filling

Precooked or fresh ground sausage

Flour

Cut precooked sausage into small bits. Wrap dough around sausage pieces; pinch edges together to seal. Place smooth side up on a greased baking sheet. Let rise, then bake in preheated 350° oven for 25 minutes. If using uncooked ground sausage, mix with enough flour to shape into small strips. Seal dough around strips and bake for 40 to 50 minutes in a 300° oven. Make sure sausage is cooked thoroughly.

Coffee Break

Coffee Cakes,
Sweet Breads,
Fried Breads,
Rolls

Káva a Láska jsou nejlepší kdyš jsou horké!

Apron with Czech saying,
"Coffee and love are best when they are hot."

Prune-Cheese Cake

2-1/3 cups all-purpose flour, divided
1 package dry yeast
3/4 cup milk
2 tablespoons sugar
2 tablespoons butter
1/2 teaspoon salt
1 egg
1 (12-ounce) can prune filling

Topping:
1-1/2 cups cream-style cottage cheese
2 tablespoons plus 2 teaspoons sugar
1 tablespoon flour
1/2 teaspoon grated lemon rind
1/4 teaspoon ground cinnamon
1 egg
1/4 cup graham cracker crumbs

In a large mixing bowl, combine 1 cup flour and yeast. Heat together the milk, sugar, butter, and salt until warm and butter is melted. Add to the dry mixture; add the

egg. Beat at low speed with a mixer for about half a minute, scraping bowl. Beat 3 minutes at high speed, then stir in by hand 1-1/3 cups flour. Place in a greased bowl and turn once. Cover and chill for at least 3 to 4 hours. When ready, pat dough evenly into a greased 15-1/2 x 10-1/2-inch baking pan, forming a ridge around the edges. Spread with the prune filling and let rise in a warm place till almost doubled. Bake at 375° about 15 minutes, then let cool slightly. To prepare topping: Combine cottage cheese, 2 tablespoons sugar, flour, grated lemon rind, and cinnamon. Beat in egg. Spread atop prune filling; sprinkle with graham cracker crumbs and 2 teaspoons sugar. Bake for 10 more minutes.

Country Buns

Juanita Loven, Guttenberg, Iowa

Juanita says her mother called these melt-in-the-mouth rolls buchticky.

Favorite kolache or sweet roll dough	Melted butter
Filling of choice	Powdered sugar
Melted shortening for brushing	

Shape equal portions of dough into buns. Flatten and place a tablespoon of filling in center of each. Fold sides over center and seal. Brush top and sides with shortening and place in greased baking pan, taking care not to place them too close together. Bake in preheated 350° oven for about 30 minutes, until golden brown. To serve, roll in melted butter and powdered sugar. (*Hint:* Keep warm in an electric skillet.)

Moravian Sugar Cake

2 packages yeast

2/3 cup lukewarm water

1/2 cup sugar

1-1/2 teaspoons salt

1 cup butter, softened, divided

1 cup milk, scalded

2 eggs, slightly beaten

5 cups sifted all-purpose flour

Cinnamon

Nutmeg

2 cups light brown sugar

Powdered sugar (optional)

Soften yeast in the water. Add the sugar, salt, and 3 tablespoons of the butter to the scalded milk. Cool to lukewarm, stirring until the sugar is dissolved. Add the yeast mixture and eggs. Add flour, 1 cup at a time to make a soft dough, and stir until blended. Turn onto a floured board and knead until smooth. Place in a greased bowl,

continued

Moravian Sugar Cake continued

grease the top, cover, and let rise in a warm place until doubled, about 1-1/4 hours. Divide raised dough into three parts and press each into a 7 x 11-inch greased baking pan (or two parts into two pans for thicker cakes). Grease surfaces, cover, and let rise again until doubled, about 30 minutes. Pinch the dough all over with the thumb and finger to make holes in it. Sprinkle lightly with the cinnamon and nutmeg and very generously with the brown sugar. Dot with bits of the remaining butter. Bake in preheated 400° oven until brown with a bubbly topping, about 20 minutes. Serve warm. Cut into squares. May be reheated to serve later. Sprinkle with powdered sugar if desired.

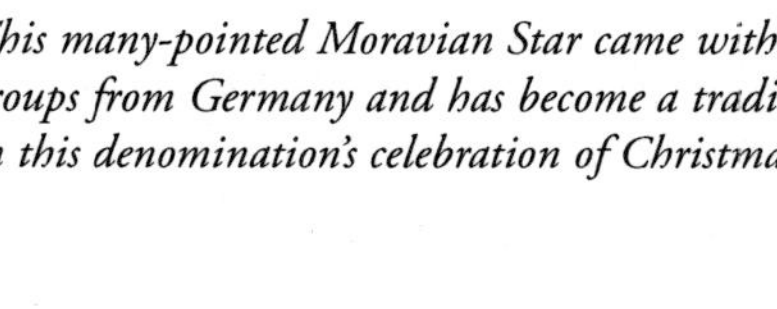

This many-pointed Moravian Star came with Moravian groups from Germany and has become a traditional symbol in this denomination's celebration of Christmas.

Poppy Seed Roll

Helen Fiala, Phillips (Wisconsin) Czechoslovakian Community Festival

1 package dry yeast
1/4 cup lukewarm water
1/2 cup plus 1 teaspoon sugar, divided
1 cup milk
1/2 cup shortening
1/2 teaspoon salt
2 eggs
3 cups flour

Poppy seed filling:
1/2 pound ground poppy seed
1/2 cup sugar
1 tablespoon lemon juice
1/2 cup honey
1/2 cup raisins, chopped
1-1/2 cups milk
2 tablespoons butter

continued

Dissolve yeast in the warm water; add 1 teaspoon of the sugar. Scald the milk and add remaining sugar, shortening, and salt. Cool to lukewarm; add the eggs, yeast mixture, and about 3 cups of the flour. Knead until smooth and satiny. Place in a lightly greased bowl and let rise until doubled. Turn out onto a floured surface and roll to 1/2-inch thickness. Prepare the filling: Mix all ingredients except butter and cook on low heat until thickened. Stir constantly and take care that mixture does not scorch. Add the butter. Cool. Spread filling over the dough. Roll up jelly-roll style and crimp edges to seal. Place in a greased Bundt pan; grease top and let rise until doubled. Bake at 350° for about 50 minutes.

Note: If you grind whole poppy seeds, put a cup of milk into a blender with the seeds. Blend for about 10 minutes or until mixture thickens. Cook as usual, adding sugar. Adjust the amount of milk if adding other liquid flavorings.

Grandma Bradnan's Nut Roll

Marion Bradnan, Columbia Station, Ohio

1 cake yeast

1/4 cup lukewarm milk

1 teaspoon plus 3 tablespoons sugar, divided

2 cups scalded milk

1 teaspoon salt

1/4 pound butter plus 1/4 pound oleo

2 egg yolks

6 cups flour

Nut filling:

2 pounds ground nuts

1/2 pound melted butter

2 cups sugar

2 teaspoons vanilla

4 egg whites

Dissolve yeast in 1/4 cup lukewarm milk; add 1 teaspoon sugar and let stand until

continued

foamy. Add the 3 tablespoons of sugar, salt, and shortenings to the scalded milk. Stir until dissolved. Cool milk mixture to lukewarm and add egg yolks and yeast mixture. Gradually add flour; blend well and beat about 2 minutes. Dough must be soft but not sticky; add a bit more flour if needed. Cover with a clean cloth and let rise until doubled, about 2 hours. Divide into five parts; roll out each in a rectangle, then spread with nut filling. Roll up jelly-roll style and shape into a round or a crescent in a large baking pan. Let rise again, then bake at 350° for 30 to 35 minutes.

Note: A poppy seed filling can be used instead of the nut filling. Be generous with the filling.

No-Rise Nut Rolls

Marcia Toth, Wadsworth, Ohio

1 pound butter
6 cups flour, extra if needed
1/2 cup granulated sugar
2 cakes yeast
1/3 cup warm water
1/2 pint sour cream

3 eggs, beaten

Nut filling:
1-1/2 pounds ground nuts
1 pound brown sugar
3 tablespoons milk

Mix butter, flour, and sugar as if for pie dough. Dissolve yeast in warm water, then add to flour mixture along with sour cream and eggs. Mix well to form a soft dough; cover and refrigerate overnight. Next day divide dough into 4 parts and on a lightly

continued

No-Rise Nut Rolls continued

floured surface, roll each part to about 1/4 inch thick. Mix together filling ingredients and spread over the dough. Roll up and place on ungreased baking sheet. Bake at 350° for 30 minutes. Makes 4 nut rolls. Slice to serve.

The custom of hanging a spider among decorations on Christmas trees originated in Germany, but spread to other parts of Central Europe. As the tale goes, in the flurry of holiday cleaning, the tiny household spiders were banished from their place on the ceiling. Curious to investigate the tree, they crept in and excitedly scurried over the tree, leaving trails of dusty, gray web. The Christ Child, seeing the happy spiders, thought of how brokenhearted the mother would be and reached out to bless the dusty web, which turned to shimmering, sparkling silver and gold. Ever since, trees may be hung with tinsel, and you may find a spider filled with wonder at the glittering beauty.

Poppy Seed Coffee Cake

Sokol Greater Cleveland Cookbook, Centennial 1997 Issue

1 package dry yeast
3/4 cup warm milk, divided
2 eggs
1/4 cup sugar
1/4 cup butter, softened
1 teaspoon salt
1 teaspoon grated lemon rind
3 cups flour, divided
1 egg, lightly beaten

Poppy seed filling:
1 cup ground poppy seed
1/2 cup sugar
1 tablespoon grated lemon rind
1 tablespoon melted butter
1 tablespoon honey
1/2 cup cake crumbs
    (or graham cracker crumbs)
1/2 cup warm milk

continued

Poppy Seed Coffee Cake continued

Raise yeast in a little of the warm milk. Beat two eggs; add sugar and softened butter. Add salt, lemon rind, remaining milk, and 1 cup flour. Mix together and add yeast mixture. Stir in rest of flour and continue mixing until dough is smooth and does not stick to bowl. Dough should be soft. In a separate bowl, mix together all ingredients for filling until smooth and of spreading consistency. On a floured surface, roll out dough into a rectangular piece, 1/2 inch thick. Spread with poppy seed filling. Roll up on long side and put into a well-greased fluted cake form. Brush with the lightly beaten egg. Let rise in a warm place until doubled. Bake at 350° for about 45 minutes.

The Hedgehog brings
Much luck to you.

In all you wish
In all you do.

Just pet him gently
Every day.

And all good things
Will come your way.

Lemon Poppy Seed Bread

Juanita Loven, Guttenberg, Iowa

4 eggs
1 package lemon cake mix with pudding
1 (3-ounce) package instant lemon
  pudding mix
1/2 cup plain yogurt
3 tablespoons poppy seed
1 cup hot water

Preheat oven to 325°. Grease two large or three small loaf pans. In a large mixing bowl, beat eggs. Stir in cake and pudding mixes, yogurt, and poppy seed. Mix together. Add hot water and mix well. Pour into pans. Bake for 50 to 60 minutes if using large pans, 40 to 50 minutes if using small pans. Remove loaves from pans to cool.

Plum Nut Bread

1 cup butter or margarine
2 cups sugar
1 teaspoon vanilla
4 eggs
3 cups flour
1 teaspoon salt
1 teaspoon cream of tartar

1/2 teaspoon baking soda
3/4 cup plain yogurt
1 teaspoon grated lemon peel
2 cups diced (1/2-inch pieces) purple prune plums
1 cup chopped walnuts

Cream together butter, sugar, and vanilla until fluffy. Add eggs, one at a time, beating after each addition. Sift flour, salt, cream of tartar, and baking soda together. Blend yogurt and lemon peel; add to the creamed mixture alternately with the dry

ingredients. Stir to blend well. Add plum pieces and nuts; mix well. Divide between two greased and floured 9 x 5-inch loaf pans. Bake at 350° for 50 to 55 minutes or until bread tests done when toothpick inserted in center comes out clean.

Glass factories began operating in Bohemia as early as the 14th century. Over the next six hundred years, Bohemian craftsmen developed important glass dyes, stains, and decorating techniques. One of the many areas in which they excelled was glass blowing.

Today, Christmas ornaments are made using glass-blowing techniques developed over a hundred years ago. Craftsmen make ornaments from traditional mold patterns and from molds reflecting more modern trends.

Blown-glass Santa Christmas ornament

Braided Loaf

Dolores Marlenga, Phillips (Wisconsin) Czechoslovakian Community Festival

2 packages dry yeast
3/4 cup plus 1 tablespoon sugar
3/4 cup warm water
3/4 cup margarine
1 cup milk, scalded
2 teaspoons salt
6 eggs
1 teaspoon vanilla
Grated lemon rind, to taste

1/2 teaspoon nutmeg
6 cups flour, more or less as needed
1 cup raisins
1/2 cup candied mixed fruit
1/2 cup candied cherries
1/4 cup sliced almonds

Egg wash:
2 egg yolks
2 tablespoons milk

In a large bowl, dissolve yeast and 1 tablespoon of the sugar in the warm water. Add remaining sugar and margarine to the scalded milk. Then add salt, eggs, vanilla, lemon rind, and nutmeg to milk mixture. Add milk mixture to the yeast mixture. Add the flour, raisins, mixed fruit, cherries, and nuts. Use enough flour to keep dough from sticking to hands. Beat until soft and smooth. Place in a greased bowl, cover, and let rise in a warm place until doubled. Turn out onto a floured surface and divide into three pieces. Roll each piece into three strands, braid, and put into greased loaf pans. Place pans in a warm place and let rise again until doubled. Beat together the egg yolks and milk. Brush loaves with the egg wash and bake at 375° for 35 to 40 minutes, until golden brown. Remove from pan and cool.

Note: Traditionally, this is baked for Easter and Christmas celebrations.

Christmas Twist

Mana Machovsky Zlatohlavek, Cedar Rapids, Iowa

4 cups flour
3/4 cup sugar, divided
1 cup warm milk, divided
1 package active dry yeast
1/2 teaspoon salt
1/2 cup butter or margarine, melted
2 eggs, slightly beaten (reserve about 2 tablespoons)

1 teaspoon vanilla extract
1 teaspoon grated lemon rind or 1/2 teaspoon lemon extract
1/2 teaspoon anise extract
1/4 cup nutmeats
1/4 cup raisins
Sliced almonds (optional)

Sift flour into a bowl. Make a well in the flour; put in 1 teaspoon sugar, 1/2 cup

warm milk, and yeast. Let stand about 5 minutes. Add remaining sugar, the salt, butter or margarine, eggs, milk, vanilla, lemon rind, and anise. Mix and beat well with a wooden spoon for about 10 minutes, then stir in the nuts and raisins. Sprinkle the top lightly with flour, cover, and let rise about 1-1/2 hours in a warm place. On a floured surface, form into a roll and divide into seven parts. Roll each piece into a strip about 12 inches long. Braid four strips together and place on a greased baking sheet (11 x 15-1/2 inches). Braid remaining three strips and place on top of the other. Cover and let rise about 20 to 25 minutes. Brush with the reserved egg. Sliced almonds may be placed on top. Bake in a preheated 350° oven for approximately 45 to 60 minutes, until golden brown. If the top is browning too quickly, place a sheet of foil on top. Best if not cut until the following day.

Holiday Fruit Bread

2 cups flour, divided
1/4 cup sugar
1 package dry yeast
1/8 teaspoon salt
1/8 teaspoon mace
1/2 cup milk
1/4 cup margarine
3 eggs, room temperature

1/2 cup raisins
1/2 to 1 cup candied fruit
1/2 cup chopped walnuts
Rum syrup:
1/2 cup sugar
1/3 cup water
2 teaspoons rum flavoring

Mix 3/4 cup of the flour with the sugar, yeast, salt, and mace. In a saucepan over low heat, warm milk and margarine. Add warm milk mixture to the flour mixture and

mix at medium speed for 2 minutes. Add the eggs, another 1/2 cup of flour, and beat 2 more minutes at high speed. Add remaining 3/4 cup flour and beat another 2 minutes at high speed. Cover and let rise in a warm place for about 1 hour or until bubbly. Add fruits and nuts. Turn into a greased and floured 2-quart Turk's-head or tube pan. Let rise for another hour until bubbly. Bake at 350° for 40 minutes. Dissolve sugar in the water and rum flavoring over low heat; keep hot. Immediately after removing from oven, prick surface of bread with a fork and pour hot rum syrup over the top. After syrup is absorbed, remove bread from pan and cool on a wire rack. Frost with powdered sugar frosting if desired.

Bohemian Coffee Cake

Irma Mouchka Kelly, Cedar Rapids, Iowa
Irma contributed this recipe in memory of her mother, Bessie R. Mouchka.

3 cups flour
1 cup granulated sugar
1 cup firmly packed brown sugar
1/2 teaspoon salt
1/2 cup butter

1 cup chopped dates
1 cup chopped nuts
1 teaspoon soda
1 cup sour milk

Mix together dry ingredients. Cut in butter until crumbly, as for pie crust. Reserve 1/2 cup. Add dates and nuts. Combine soda and sour milk; add to mixture. Put in a 9 x 13-inch greased pan, sprinkle with reserved butter crumbs, and bake at 350° for 1 hour.

Two-Filling Double Roll *(Plutska)*

Albert Etzel, Marion, Iowa

1 package yeast
1/2 cup lukewarm water
1/2 cup butter, melted, lightly browned
1/2 cup sugar
1 tablespoon vanilla
3 small or 2 large eggs
1-1/2 cups milk

6-1/2 cups flour
1 teaspoon salt
1 or 2 tablespoons butter, melted (not browned)

Filling:
1 (12-ounce) can cherry pie filling
1 (12-ounce) can poppy seed filling

Dissolve yeast in the warm water. Cream together butter, sugar, vanilla, and eggs. Add milk, yeast, flour, and salt. Beat well, then knead for several minutes. Place in a

continued

Two-Filling Double Roll (Plutska) *continued*

greased bowl and let rise until doubled. Punch down and refrigerate overnight. Next morning, on a floured surface, roll out into a rectangle about 1/4 inch thick and 12 inches wide. Place on a large, greased baking sheet or jelly roll pan; spread a row of filling down each side of dough, about 3 inches in from edges. Lap edges over the fillings and pinch together. Make knife slits down each fold to release steam as it bakes. Brush with melted butter and let rise about 1 hour. Bake at 350° for 35 minutes, until lightly browned. Frost if desired.

Note: Albert uses the cherry and poppy seed filling, but any combination of filling may be used (prune, apricot, etc.).

Bohemian Biscuits *(Vdolky)*

Bernice Polacek, Phillips (Wisconsin) Czechoslovakian Community Festival
A variation of this recipe is served at the hospitality table during festival time.

4-1/2 to 5 cups flour, divided
1-1/4 tablespoons dry yeast
1-1/4 cups warm milk
2 eggs
1/3 cup sugar

1 teaspoon salt
2/3 cup vegetable oil
Stewed fruit, cottage cheese, whipped
cream, cinnamon and sugar, or
other toppings of choice

Put 2 cups flour into a large bowl. Dissolve yeast in the warm milk and add to the flour. Mix thoroughly, then add eggs, sugar, salt, and oil. Beat several minutes by hand. Beat in remaining flour. Cover and let rise in a warm oven for 1 hour. Form

continued

Bohemian Biscuits (Vdolky) *continued*

balls of dough, then shape with fingers until quite thin and about 3 to 4 inches in diameter. Put on a lightly greased hot griddle and brown both sides. Cool on a rack. Spread with toppings of choice and sprinkle with cinnamon and sugar.

Note: These may also be deep-fried as for doughnuts.

Handmade in the Czech Republic

Czech Leaves *(Listy)*

Lucille Goetz, Franklin Park, Illinois

Lucille recalls Listy *made by Mother and Grandma, Chicago, 1930s and '40s.*

3 egg yolks
2 tablespoons powdered sugar
3 tablespoons cream

1 cup flour, approximately
Shortening for deep-frying

Beat egg yolks; add the sugar and cream and mix well. Gradually add the flour and work into a smooth dough. Divide dough into two parts and roll out each one very thin as for noodles. Cut into 3 x 3-inch squares and cut a 1/4-inch slit in the center of each. Deep-fry in hot shortening, turning once until golden brown. Place on paper towels to drain and cool. Dust with additional powdered sugar to serve.

Love Knots *(Listy)*

Sally Moravek, Phillips (Wisconsin) Czechoslovakian Community Festival

1/2 teaspoon salt
5 egg yolks
3 tablespoons sugar
1 tablespoon light rum

5 tablespoons sour cream
2-1/2 cups flour
Powdered sugar for dusting

Add salt to eggs and beat until lemon colored. Add sugar and rum; continue to beat. Add sour cream and flour alternately, mixing well after each addition. Knead on lightly floured surface until dough blisters. Cut in half and roll each piece very thin. Cut into 2 x 4-inch strips; make a slit in center and pull dough through slot. Fry in deep, hot fat until lightly browned. Drain and dust with powdered sugar.

Cinnamon Sugar Knots

Barbara Edmunds, Cedar Rapids, Iowa

2 cups milk
1/2 cup sugar
1/2 cup butter
1-1/2 teaspoons salt
6 cups flour, divided

2 packages dry yeast
2 eggs plus 2 egg yolks
Melted butter for dipping
Cinnamon, sugar, and grated coconut, combined for coating

Measure milk, sugar, butter, and salt in a pan and heat to warm (120°–130°). Measure 3 cups flour in a large bowl; mix in dry yeast. Add warm milk mixture and beat in eggs. Beat 1/2 minute at low speed, 3 minutes on high. Gradually mix in remaining 3 cups flour, using a wooden spoon as batter thickens. Cover and let rise

continued

Cinnamon Sugar Knots continued

in a warm place until doubled. When dough has risen, use right away or it can be refrigerated overnight. Do not knead. To make cinnamon sugar knots: Pinch off small amounts of dough; roll on lightly floured surface to a cigar-size and shape. Dip in melted butter, then in the mixture of cinnamon, sugar, and coconut. Tie dough in a loose knot. Place on foiled-lined baking sheet and let rise again until doubled. Bake at 350° until lightly browned, about 12 to 15 minutes, but watch carefully. Frost with a light sugar frosting while hot, if desired.

Note: This dough also works well for braided *Houska.*

Kraslice, *painted egg by Marj Nejdl, Master Folk Artist*

Raised Potato Doughnuts

Juanita Loven, Guttenberg, Iowa

1 cup mashed potatoes
1/3 cup shortening
2 eggs, well beaten
1/3 cup sugar
1-1/2 cups scalded milk
2 yeast cakes
4-1/2 to 5 cups flour
1 teaspoon salt

Lard or shortening for frying

Glaze for doughnuts:
1 pound powdered sugar
2 tablespoons cornstarch
1 heaping tablespoon butter
1 tablespoon sweet cream
1 teaspoon vanilla
Enough water to make a liquid glaze

Put potatoes in mixing bowl; add shortening, eggs, sugar, and hot scalded milk.

continued

When mixture is lukewarm, add crumbled yeast and let dissolve until foam rises to the top. Then add flour and salt and mix until dough is smooth. Cover and let rise in a warm place until doubled. Punch down and let rise again. Roll dough out to about 1/2 inch thick. Cut with a doughnut cutter or rim of a glass dipped in flour, but DO NOT cut out center hole. Let rise until doubled in size. When ready to fry, poke hole in the center with your finger, stretching to a size of a half-dollar. Fry in deep fat (365°) until golden brown; turn to fry other side. Remove from fat; drain and dip in glaze while warm. Prepare the glaze in a saucepan or double boiler; stir together and heat all ingredients until mixture is thickened and incorporated. Dip hot doughnuts in the glaze and place on racks to drip and cool.

Luscious Cakes

Lamb cake and cake molds

Easter Lamb Cake

Inez Michek, Phillips (Wisconsin) Czechoslovakian Community Festival

1/2 cup butter
3/4 cup sugar
3 eggs, separated
1/4 cup milk
1-1/4 cups cake flour

1/4 teaspoon salt
1-1/2 teaspoons baking soda
1/4 cup raisins (optional)
1/4 teaspoon lemon extract
Shredded coconut, white icing

Cream butter, sugar, and egg yolks. Add milk and dry ingredients. Add raisins if using. Fold in egg whites and lemon extract. Pour into greased lamb form and bake at 350° for 45 minutes. Frost with a white frosting and sprinkle with coconut; add raisins for eyes. Use small candied eggs or jelly beans to decorate around the cake.

Applesauce Cake

Phillips (Wisconsin) Czechoslovakian Community Festival

1/2 cup butter or shortening
1 cup brown sugar
1-1/2 cups flour
1 teaspoon soda
1 teaspoon cocoa

1/2 teaspoon cinnamon
1 cup unsweetened applesauce
1 cup raisins
1/2 cup chopped nutmeats

Cream butter; add brown sugar. Sift together flour, soda, cocoa, and cinnamon. Add applesauce, raisins, and nuts and mix until blended. Pour into a greased 9 x 9-inch baking pan. Bake at 350° for 40 minutes or until tests done. Serve plain or with whipped or ice cream.

Apple Pie Cake

Phillips (Wisconsin) Czechoslovakian Community Festival

1/4 cup sugar

1/4 cup butter or other shortening

1 egg

1/4 teaspoon salt

1 cup flour

1 teaspoon nutmeg

1 teaspoon cinnamon

1 teaspoon soda

1/2 cup nutmeats

2-1/2 cups dried apples*

2 teaspoons hot water

1/2 teaspoon vanilla

Hard sauce:

1/2 cup sugar

1-1/2 tablespoons flour

1 cup boiling water

1 tablespoon butter

1 teaspoon vanilla

Cream sugar and butter; mix in egg. Stir dry ingredients together and add to sugar mixture. Stir in nuts, apples, water, and vanilla. Pat into a greased 9-inch-square baking pan. Bake at 350° for 45 minutes. Serve with hard sauce.

Hard sauce: Mix sugar and flour in a saucepan. Add boiling water; bring to a boil and cook, stirring constantly for 5 minutes. Remove from heat and add butter and vanilla.

*May substitute fresh, peeled and diced apples.

Caraway Cake

Sally Moravek, Phillips (Wisconsin) Czechoslovakian Community Festival

5 eggs, separated
1/4 teaspoon salt
1-1/4 cups sugar, divided
1 cup butter or margarine, softened

1-2/3 cups cake flour
2 teaspoons caraway seed
1 teaspoon lemon extract
Powdered sugar

Beat egg whites and salt until foamy. Gradually beat in 1/2 cup sugar until peaks form; set aside. In a separate bowl, cream butter and remaining sugar until light. Beat in egg yolks one at a time. Add flour, caraway seed, and lemon extract. Mix well. Fold in egg white mixture. Spoon into a greased tube pan and bake at 300° for 65 to 70 minutes. Dust with powdered sugar before serving.

Surprise Sauerkraut Cake

2/3 cup butter
1-1/2 cups sugar
3 eggs, beaten
1 teaspoon vanilla
2-1/2 cups flour
1 teaspoon baking powder
1 teaspoon baking soda
1/2 cup cocoa
1/4 teaspoon salt
1 cup water

2/3 cup sauerkraut, washed, drained,
    finely chopped

Icing:
1-1/2 squares unsweetened chocolate
1/4 cup butter
1/4 teaspoon salt
3 cups sifted powdered sugar
4 to 5 tablespoons hot scalded cream or
    milk
1 teaspoon vanilla

continued

Surprise Sauerkraut Cake continued

Cream butter and sugar thoroughly. Add eggs and vanilla. Sift together the flour, baking powder, soda, cocoa, and salt, and add alternately with the water to the creamed mixture, beating well. Add sauerkraut and stir to blend. Bake in two 8-inch greased layer pans in a 350° oven for 30 minutes. Cool before icing.

Icing: Melt chocolate squares and set aside. Cream butter and salt. Blend in powdered sugar alternately with scalded cream or milk. Add vanilla and the melted chocolate. Thin with additional cream if necessary.

Blown-glass musical instruments represent the joy of music and singing during the holiday season.

—In the collection of the museum store of the National Czech & Slovak Museum & Library

Poppy Seed Crown Cake

Emily Palka, Phillips (Wisconsin) Czechoslovakian Community Festival

1 cup ground poppy seed
1-1/2 cups milk, divided
1/2 cup butter
1-1/2 cups sugar

2 eggs, separated
2 cups flour
2 teaspoons baking powder
2 egg whites, beaten stiff

Boil poppy seed in 3/4 cup of the milk; let stand overnight. Next day, cream butter and sugar; add milk-soaked poppy seed mixture and egg yolks. Sift flour and baking powder together; add to creamed mixture. Slowly add 3/4 cup of milk and mix well. Beat egg whites until stiff and fold into mixture. Pour batter into a buttered tube pan; bake at 375° for 45 minutes. (May use four beaten egg whites instead of two yolks.)

Poppy Seed Crown Cake with Filling

Marcia Toth, Wadsworth, Ohio

The following variation for baking and filling calls for the four egg-white batter.

Batter using 4 egg whites (page 93)

Filling:

3/4 cup milk

2 tablespoons butter

4 egg yolks

1/2 cup sugar

Pinch of salt

Bake batter in two 9-inch layer cake pans at 350° for 30 minutes. To prepare filling, scald milk and butter together. Beat egg yolks; add sugar and salt. Combine with hot milk and cook until bubbly. Add a little cornstarch dissolved in water if thicker filling is desired. Cool and spread between cooled cake layers.

Poppy Seed Cake with Lemon Filling

1/2 cup ground poppy seed
3/4 cup milk
3/4 cup butter
1-1/2 cups sugar
2 cups cake flour
2 teaspoons baking powder
1/4 teaspoon salt
4 beaten egg whites

Lemon filling:
1/2 cup sugar
2 tablespoons cornstarch
1/2 cup cold water

2 teaspoons grated lemon peel
1 beaten egg yolk
3 tablespoons lemon juice
1 tablespoon butter

Fluffy frosting:
4 tablespoons flour
1 cup milk
1/2 cup butter plus 1/2 cup Crisco
1/4 teaspoon salt
1 cup granulated sugar
2 teaspoons vanilla

continued

Poppy Seed Cake with Lemon Filling continued

Soak poppy seed in the milk for about 2 hours. Cream butter and sugar. Sift together: cake flour, baking powder, and salt. Add dry mixture alternately with the poppy seed and milk mixture to the creamed mixture. Combine until smooth, then fold in beaten egg whites. Place batter in a greased 9 x 13-inch pan. Bake in preheated 350° oven for 30 to 35 minutes.

Lemon filling: Mix sugar and cornstarch in the cold water. Add lemon peel. Cook and stir over low heat until thick and clear. Combine egg yolk, lemon juice, and butter and slowly stir into the hot sugar mixture. Cook and stir for about 2 minutes. Cool and spread over cooled cake.

Top with fluffy frosting: Cook flour and milk until thick. Cool. Cream butter, shortening (may use margarine in place of Crisco), and salt together for about 4 minutes; gradually add sugar and beat 4 minutes. Add flour mixture and vanilla. Beat 4 minutes more.

Poppy Seed Cake

Bernice Polacek, Phillips (Wisconsin) Czechoslovakian Community Festival

This cake has been served at the hospitality table during the festival.

3 cups flour
2 cups sugar
1-1/2 cups salad oil
4 eggs

1 teaspoon vanilla
1-1/2 teaspoons baking soda
1 (14-ounce) can Solo poppy seed filling
1 cup chopped pecans

Mix together all ingredients until smooth. Beat well with mixer on medium speed for 2 minutes. Pour into a heavy, lightly greased Bundt pan or a 10-inch angel food pan. (Must be a tube pan.) Bake 350° for 1 hour and 10 minutes. Cool before removing from pan.

Poppy Seed Torte

7 large eggs, separated
1 cup sugar
1 cup sifted cake flour
1/4 cup cold water mixed with
    1 teaspoon vanilla
1/2 teaspoon cream of tartar
1/4 teaspoon salt
3/4 cup poppy seed

Fluffy custard:
3/4 cup milk
2 tablespoons flour
3/4 cup butter
3/4 cup superfine sugar
1/8 teaspoon salt
1 teaspoon vanilla

In a large bowl, beat egg yolks, on high speed, until lemon colored. Gradually beat in sugar until mixture is thick and ivory colored. Add flour, water/vanilla mixture

and beat, at lowest speed, just until smooth. Clean beaters. In a separate bowl, beat egg whites, cream of tartar, and salt until stiff. By hand, fold the yolk mixture into egg whites, then fold in poppy seed. Turn into an ungreased 10-inch angel food cake pan and bake at 325° for 1 hour. Invert pan and let cool. When cool, loosen sides to remove from pan. Cut in half crosswise; place bottom half on a cake plate and spread with half the fluffy custard. Add top half and spread with remaining custard. Sprinkle with extra poppy seed.

Fluffy custard: In a small saucepan, gradually stir milk into flour until smooth. Cook over moderately low heat, stirring constantly until thickened and boiling. Cool until just warm to the touch. Beat butter until creamy, then gradually add and beat in sugar. Add cooled milk mixture, salt, and vanilla. Beat until fluffy.

Raisin-Nut Gingerbread

1 cup white sugar
1/2 cup butter
3 eggs
1 cup dark corn syrup
3 cups sifted flour
1/2 teaspoon soda
2 teaspoons baking powder

1 teaspoon cinnamon
1/2 teaspoon ground ginger
1/2 teaspoon ground cloves
1 cup milk
1 cup raisins
1/2 cup chopped nuts

Cream sugar and butter. Add eggs and syrup; beat well, then set aside. In a separate bowl, sift the flour and measure. Add the soda, baking powder, and spices and sift once more. Add the flour mixture and the milk to the creamed mixture and beat for

1 minute. Toss raisins and nuts to coat with a little flour, then mix into batter. Bake in a greased 9 x 13-inch pan for 30 to 35 minutes at 350°.

Artifacts seen in the
19th-Century Immigrant Home at the
National Czech & Slovak Museum & Library,
Cedar Rapids, Iowa

Rhubarb Gingerbread

Frank Edmunds, Cedar Rapids, Iowa

1-1/2 cups chopped rhubarb
   (about 1/2 pound)
Sugar
2-1/4 cups flour
1 teaspoon ground ginger
1 teaspoon baking soda
1/2 teaspoon ground allspice

1/2 teaspoon ground cloves
1/4 teaspoon salt
1/2 cup butter
1 cup molasses
2 tablespoons brown sugar
1 egg
1 cup boiling water

Toss rhubarb with enough sugar to coat. Set aside. Mix together flour, ginger, soda, and spices and set aside. Cream butter, molasses, and brown sugar. Beat in egg and

blend well. Add boiling water alternately with the flour mixture and stir until smooth. Pour half the batter into a greased and floured 9 x 5-inch loaf pan. Spread rhubarb on top of batter and top with remaining batter. Bake at 350° for 55 to 60 minutes or until cake tests done. Cool in pan for about 10 minutes, then turn out on rack to cool completely. Slices more easily if refrigerated.

Flags

Slovak Republic, United States, Czech Republic

Czech Plum Cake

Frank Edmunds, Cedar Rapids, Iowa

1 cup sugar plus 2 tablespoons, divided
3/4 cup butter
2 eggs
2 cups flour
1/4 teaspoon baking powder

1 tablespoon lemon juice
1/2 teaspoon vanilla
1-1/2 pounds prune plums
1 teaspoon cinnamon
Whipped cream

Cut 1/2 cup sugar into the butter. Mix together well. Add eggs and beat into sugar mixture until light, about 5 minutes. Gradually beat in flour and baking powder. Add lemon juice and vanilla. Cut plums in half, remove pits, and mix with 1/2 cup sugar and cinnamon. Butter a 9 x 13-inch baking pan, fill evenly with the batter. Space

plum halves, cut side up, over the batter. Sprinkle with the 2 tablespoons of sugar. Bake in preheated 350° oven for about 30 minutes or until tests done. Serve in large squares with a dollop of whipped cream.

Note: The juice of the fruit will soak into the pastry to color and flavor the cake. Cherries, strawberries, apricots, or other fruits of choice may be used.

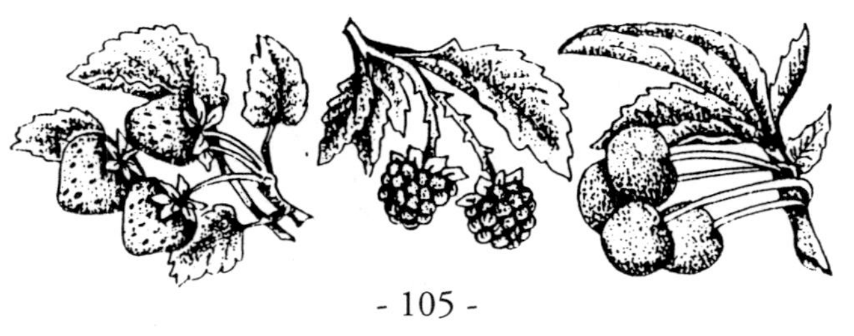

Baba Au Rum

4 egg yolks
2 tablespoons sugar
1/2 cup softened sweet butter
3 cups flour
1 teaspoon salt
2 teaspoons baking powder
3/4 cup warm milk

1 teaspoon grated orange rind
Syrup:
1 cup sugar
1/2 cup water
3 tablespoons rum
1/4 cup orange juice

Beat egg yolks, sugar, and butter until thick and fluffy. Mix flour, salt, and baking powder. Alternately beat in the flour mixture and milk. Add orange rind. Pour into a greased Bundt pan and bake at 350° for 45 minutes. Meanwhile, cook sugar and

water until clear and thick. Cool slightly and stir in rum and orange juice. Loosen sides of cake; invert to remove from pan. Place cake on a platter and pour syrup over while still hot. Let cool thoroughly before cutting.

Modra ceramic plate combines beauty with practicality. Crafted by Slovak artisans in the tradition of some of Eastern Europe's oldest ceramists, the Habaner, this is a fine example of the region's valued folk art form.
—In the collection of the museum store of National Czech & Slovak Museum & Library

Coffee *(Kava)* Cake

6 eggs, separated
2 cups powdered sugar
1/3 cup very strong prepared coffee
1 stick butter, melted
1-3/4 cups flour
1/4 teaspoon baking powder
Filling:
1 cup milk

1 tablespoon instant coffee powder
1 cup powdered sugar
1 tablespoon cornstarch
2 egg yolks
1 tablespoon vanilla
2 sticks butter, melted
2 tablespoons rum

In a large bowl, mix egg yolks and powdered sugar. While mixing thoroughly, add coffee and butter. In another bowl, beat egg whites until the consistency of whipped

cream. In a third bowl, mix flour and baking powder, and slowly fold into the egg whites, then slowly fold this mixture into the egg yolk mixture. Pour batter into two 8-inch round, greased cake pans. Bake at 350° for 40 minutes. After cakes have cooled, remove from pans and place on platters to cool thoroughly. While cakes are cooling, prepare the filling. Heat milk and dissolve instant coffee. Add sugar, boil for 4 minutes, and set aside to cool. In a small bowl, mix cornstarch, egg yolks, and vanilla. Add to cooled milk mixture, then add melted butter and rum. Allow to cool thoroughly. Spread filling on each cake layer and stack.

Prune Cake

1-1/4 cups sugar
1/2 cup butter
2 eggs, well beaten
1 cup stewed prunes with juice
6 tablespoons sour cream
2 cups flour
1 teaspoon soda
1 teaspoon cinnamon
1 teaspoon nutmeg
1/4 teaspoon ground cloves

1 teaspoon vanilla
White icing of choice
Filling:
1/2 cup sugar
1/2 cup sour cream
1/2 cup raisins
1/2 cup nutmeats
1 teaspoon flour
1 egg
1/4 teaspoon vanilla

Cream sugar and butter. Beat in eggs. Stir in remaining ingredients. Bake in two 9-inch round layer tins at 350° for 30 to 35 minutes or until tests done. Cool slightly before removing from pans. Cool each layer thoroughly before filling.

Filling: Mix all ingredients together and cook until thick. Cool and spread between cake layers, then frost top and sides of cake with a fluffy white icing of choice.

Note: This cake can be baked in a 9 x 13-inch pan without the filling. Frost as desired.

From Borsice

Dolls made in the Czech Republic

From Zdiar

Molasses Cookies

Anna Peroutka, Phillips (Wisconsin) Czechoslovakian Community Festival

1 cup shortening

1 cup brown sugar

2 eggs

1 cup molasses

5 cups flour

1/2 teaspoon salt

1 teaspoon baking soda

1 teaspoon ginger

1 teaspoon cinnamon

Raspberry jam

Cream shortening and sugar; add eggs and molasses. Sift dry ingredients together. Add to creamed mixture. Refrigerate dough. Roll out on floured surface to 1/8-inch thickness. Cut out with large round cutter. Put 1 teaspoonful of jam on one half, fold over, and crimp edges with a fork. Bake on greased cookie sheet at 350° for 12 to 15 minutes. Glaze with a powdered sugar icing if desired.

Honey Cookies

1/2 cup margarine
1/2 cup honey
1 egg
1-1/4 cups flour
1/2 teaspoon baking soda

1/2 teaspoon salt
1/2 cup chocolate chips (optional)
1/2 teaspoon vanilla
1/2 cup chopped nuts

Cream margarine and honey. Add egg and beat well. Sift dry ingredients together and add to creamed mixture. Add chocolate chips (if desired), vanilla, and nuts. Mix well. Drop by rounded teaspoonfuls onto greased cookie sheet. Bake at 375° about 10 minutes. Makes about 3 dozen.

Filbert Nut Mounds

Mana Machovsky Zlatohlavek, Cedar Rapids, Iowa

1 egg white (large)
2/3 cup sugar
1 tablespoon lemon juice

1-1/2 cups lightly packed ground
filberts

In a medium-sized bowl stir egg white with a fork. Add sugar gradually and mix well. Add lemon juice and nuts and mix. Drop by rounded teaspoonfuls on a greased cookie sheet and bake at 350° for 20 to 25 minutes. Will be a very light pink when done. Remove from cookie sheet immediately.

Filbert Crescents

Mana Machovsky Zlatohlavek, Cedar Rapids, Iowa

1 cup soft butter
1/4 cup sugar
2 cups sifted flour

1 cup ground filberts
1 teaspoon vanilla
Powdered sugar

Cream butter and sugar until light and fluffy. Add remaining ingredients except powdered sugar and mix well. Chill. Shape into tiny rolls and form into crescents on a lightly greased cookie sheet. Bake at 350° for 10 minutes. Do not bake until browned. Roll in powdered sugar and store in an air-tight container. Makes 8 to 10 dozen.

Pecan Kisses

Mana Machovsky Zlatohlavek, Cedar Rapids, Iowa

2 egg whites
1/8 teaspoon salt
2 cups sifted powdered sugar

1 teaspoon vinegar
1 teaspoon vanilla
1 cup pecan pieces

Beat egg whites and the salt until soft peaks form. Gradually beat in sugar, vinegar, and vanilla and continue beating until very stiff. Fold in pecans. Drop by teaspoonfuls onto a greased baking sheet. Bake at 300° for 15 to 20 minutes or until firm. Cookies should remain light colored. Cool on racks. Makes about 3 dozen.

Pecan Shorts

Mana Machovsky Zlatohlavek, Cedar Rapids, Iowa

1/2 cup butter
1/4 cup sifted powdered sugar
1/2 teaspoon vanilla
1-1/2 teaspoons cold water

1 cup sifted flour
1 cup chopped pecans
Powdered sugar

Cream butter, then add sugar and mix until light and fluffy. Add vanilla, water, and flour. Stir well. Add nuts and mix thoroughly. Shape into a long roll and chill for at least 2 hours. Slice and bake on a greased cookie sheet about 10 to 12 minutes at 325°. While warm, roll in powdered sugar. Makes about 1-1/2 dozen.

Nut Crescents

Toni Birmingham, Phillips (Wisconsin) Czechoslovakian Community Festival

4 cups all-purpose flour
1 pound margarine, softened
2 (8-ounce) packages cream cheese,
  softened

Filling:
1 cup egg whites
1 pound powdered sugar
2 teaspoons vanilla
1 pound ground walnuts

In a large bowl, mix flour, margarine, and cream cheese with hands until smooth. Form into walnut-size balls. Layer in a large pan; separate layers with waxed paper. Cover and refrigerate overnight. To prepare filling, beat egg whites to form peaks. Gradually add powdered sugar, beating until stiff. Add vanilla and fold in nuts.

continued

Working with six at a time, roll each very thin on a surface dusted with powdered sugar. Spread with thin layer of filling and roll into a crescent. Place on well-greased cookie sheet and bake at 375° for 8 to 10 minutes. They will be very light in color. Cool on racks.

Note: Juanita Loven's version of a similar recipe in smaller quantity suggests dividing dough into balls large enough to roll into a 9-inch circle; cut into nine wedges. Place a teaspoon of filling on each wedge and roll into a crescent. Bake at 325° for 20 to 25 minutes. Sprinkle with powdered sugar. Juanita's nut filling: Heat 1/2 cup milk and stir in 1 tablespoon butter, 1 pound finely chopped walnuts or pecans, 1 teaspoon lemon juice, and 1 cup sugar. Cool before filling crescents.

Nut Kifles

Cindy Babroski, Oviedo, Florida

1 pound butter
4 cups all-purpose flour
3 eggs, separated

1-1/2 cups sour cream
1-1/2 cups ground nuts
1-1/2 cups sugar

Cut butter into flour as for pie dough. Beat egg yolks and sour cream together, then add to flour mixture. Mix well. Divide dough into six parts. Wrap in waxed paper and chill for at least 6 hours. Roll each piece on a floured surface into a 12-inch circle; cut evenly into twelve wedges. Brush each with unbeaten egg white and sprinkle with combined nuts and sugar. Roll wedge from wide end to form a crescent. Dip in egg white, then nut mixture. Bake on ungreased cookie sheet at 350°, 15 to 20 minutes or until lightly browned.

Nut Squares

Cindy Babroski, Oviedo, Florida

2 eggs
2 cups brown sugar
1 teaspoon vanilla
1 cup flour

1 teaspoon salt
1/4 teaspoon soda
2 cups chopped nuts

Beat eggs in a bowl; add brown sugar and vanilla. Sift together flour, salt, and soda. Add to egg mixture. Blend in nuts. Bake in an 8 x 8-inch greased pan for 35 minutes at 350°. Cut into squares.

Nut Horns

Cindy Babroski, Oviedo, Florida

2-1/2 cups flour
1 package yeast
1/2 pound butter
3 egg yolks
1/2 pint sour cream

Nut mixture:
1 pound ground walnuts
1 cup granulated sugar
1/2 cup brown sugar

Sift flour; sprinkle yeast over flour. Cut in butter as for pie dough. Add egg yolks and sour cream. Mix well and chill overnight. Stir ingredients for nut mixture together, then sprinkle amounts as used on a board. Shape small pieces of dough into balls; flatten by pressing into nut mixture on board, then roll into a crescent. Place on a cookie sheet and bake at 350° for 25 minutes or until golden brown.

Refrigerated Horns

Sokol Greater Cleveland Cookbook, Centennial 1997 Issue

Dough:

1 package dry yeast
1/2 pint sour cream
3 egg yolks
1 teaspoon vanilla
1 pound stick margarine, softened
5 cups unsifted flour
   (Sapphire if available)

Filling:

1/2 pound ground walnuts
1/2 pound ground pecans
1 stick butter, melted
1/2 cup sugar
1/4 cup honey
1 teaspoon vanilla
Confectioner's sugar

Mix together yeast and sour cream, then beat in egg yolks and vanilla. Stir in margarine. Using hands, mix in flour. Form dough into 8 patties (hamburger size). Wrap

each patty in waxed paper or foil. Refrigerate overnight. Mix nuts, butter, sugar, honey, and vanilla for filling. Makes about 3 cups. Divide filling into 8 parts; use 1 part per patty of dough. Sprinkle confectioner's sugar on a board and roll out 1 patty of dough into a round 1/8 inch thick. Cut round into 16 wedges. Place 1 teaspoon filling on wide end of each wedge and roll up like a crescent roll. Place point down on ungreased cookie sheet. Bake in preheated 350° oven for about 15 minutes or until light brown. Cool on racks and sprinkle with confectioner's sugar when cool.

Note: Lenora Jelinek Watson, Cedar Rapids, submitted a similar recipe, *Rohlícky,* with some variation in ingredients (no sour cream, more eggs). Lenora notes that she still makes these following the method used by her mother in the 1920s–30s. Dough is wrapped in a towel and soaked in cold water to chill. Finished *Rohlícky* are often hung on the Christmas tree, but are good anytime.

Bohemian Chocolate Cookies

Lucille Goetz, Franklin Park, Illinois

1/2 cup butter
1/2 cup vegetable shortening
1-1/4 cups powdered sugar
1 teaspoon vanilla
1-1/4 cups sifted flour

Dash of salt
6 ounces sweet milk chocolate, ground
   or finely grated
1 cup ground walnuts

Cream shortenings; add sugar and cream together until light and fluffy. Add remaining ingredients and mix well. Shape into 1-inch balls and place on ungreased cookie sheet. Bake 12 minutes at 375°. Makes about 5 dozen.

Bohemian Form Cookies *(Prasny)*

Lucille Goetz, Franklin Park, Illinois

Prasny *pans are similar to tartlet tins.*

1 teaspoon salt

1 teaspoon cinnamon

1 teaspoon ground cloves

1 teaspoon cocoa

4 cups sifted flour

2 cups butter or other shortening

2 cups sugar

2 eggs

1 cup ground almonds or walnut

Add salt, spices, and cocoa to the sifted flour and sift together. Cream butter; gradually add sugar and beat mixture until light and fluffy. Add eggs one at a time, beating well after each. Stir in ground nuts, then add dry ingredients to form a

continued

Bohemian Form Cookies (Prasny) *continued*

dough. Pinch off small balls of dough, place in center of ungreased *prasny* pans, and press with fingers to completely line shell. Care should be taken to cover the bottom as thinly as possible. Place dough-lined forms on cookie sheet and bake at 350° about 15 minutes or until delicately browned. Remove to cool on wire racks, turning cookies over so that the pattern is on top. A light squeeze of the *prasny* shell will release the baked cookie.

Note: If forms are not available, form dough into walnut-size balls. Place an inch apart on an ungreased cookie sheet and bake 10 to 15 minutes. Balls can be pressed with a decorative cookie stamp to a form a design on top.

Kolache Cookies

Fern Kaplan Fackler, Cedar Rapids, Iowa

2-1/4 cups flour	1 cup butter
3/4 cup sugar	1 egg
1/4 teaspoon baking powder	1 teaspoon vanilla extract
1/2 teaspoon salt	Prepared poppy seed or apricot filling

Sift dry ingredients together. Cut in butter until mixture is in fine lumps. Measure egg in measuring cup; if necessary, add enough water to make 1/4 cup. Add egg and vanilla to flour mixture and beat well. Form into balls or use a cookie press to make a round shape. Make an indentation (use top of vanilla bottle dipped in flour) in the top of each cookie. Fill with choice of filling. Bake at 375°, 10 to 15 minutes.

Hermits

Marion Bradnan, Columbia Station, Ohio

1 cup shortening

2 cups brown sugar

2 eggs

1/2 cup cold coffee

3-1/2 cups flour

1 teaspoon soda

1 teaspoon salt

1 teaspoon nutmeg

1 teaspoon cinnamon

2-1/2 cups chopped dates

1-1/4 cups broken walnuts

Cream shortening, sugar, and eggs. Add coffee, then sift in combined flour, soda, salt, nutmeg, and cinnamon. Mix together, then blend in dates and walnuts. Drop rounded teaspoonfuls about 2 inches apart on a lightly greased baking sheet. Bake at 400° for 8 to 10 minutes.

Rhubarb Crisp

Carol McLaughlin, Phillips (Wisconsin) Czechoslovakian Community Festival

1 cup flour
3/4 cup oatmeal
1 cup brown sugar
1/2 cup butter
1/2 teaspoon cinnamon
4 to 5 cups diced rhubarb

Syrup:
1 cup sugar
1 cup water
1 teaspoon vanilla
2 tablespoons cornstarch

Mix all ingredients for crust until crumbly. Press 1/2 of mixture into 9 x 13-inch pan. Spread diced rhubarb over crust. Combine syrup ingredients and cook over low heat until thick. Pour hot syrup over rhubarb; sprinkle with remaining crumbs. Bake at 350° for 30 minutes. When cool, cut into squares.

Apricot Squares

Mrs. Ed Pavoucek, Bellevue, Nebraska

1-1/2 cups flour
1/2 cup sugar
1 teaspoon baking powder
1/8 teaspoon salt
1/4 cup butter
1 egg, plus 1 yolk (reserve egg white)

1/3 cup cream
1 cup apricot preserves
Topping:
2 tablespoons flour
1-1/2 tablespoons sugar
1 tablespoon butter

Mix dry ingredients together. Cut in butter as for pie crust. Blend one egg and the cream together and combine with flour mixture. Form dough into two long rolls and chill overnight. Grease and flour a jelly roll pan or cookie sheet. Roll out one roll of

dough into a 9-inch square. Place in jelly roll pan or on cookie sheet and cover with preserves. Roll second layer and place over preserves. Mix ingredients for topping together. Brush top layer of dough with the reserved egg white and sprinkle with the topping. Bake at 350° for 25 to 30 minutes or until lightly browned.

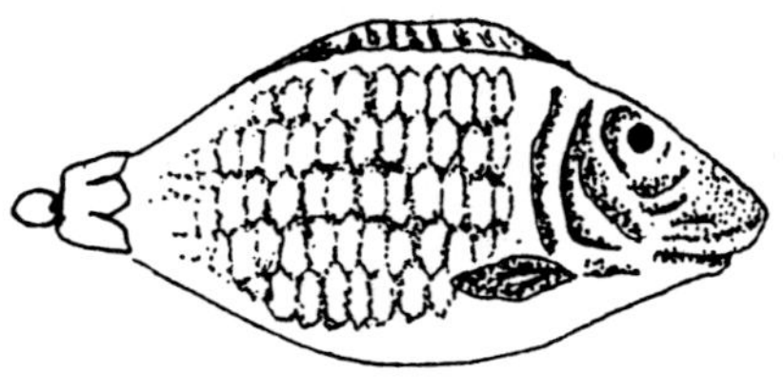

Blown-glass Christmas carp ornament

Mother Brazda's Cherry or Berry Squares

Lillian Kopecky, Cedar Rapids, Iowa

4 tablespoons butter

1 cup sugar

1/2 cup plus 2 tablespoons milk

1 egg

1 teaspoon vanilla

Grated rind from 1 lemon

4 cups flour

2 teaspoons baking powder

Cherry or berry preserves of choice

Cream together butter and sugar; add milk, egg, vanilla, and lemon rind. Mix in flour and baking powder to form a dough. Divide dough in half. Work one half to fit bottom of a greased 9 x 13-inch pan. Cover with preserves of choice. Roll out other half on lightly floured surface; cut into strips and form crosswork pattern over preserves. Bake at 400° until edges are lightly browned, about 20 minutes; watch carefully.

Apple Strudel

Juanita Loven, Guttenberg, Iowa

1/2 cup butter or margarine
3 cups sifted flour
1/2 teaspoon salt
3/4 cup warm water
1 egg, slightly beaten

1 cup sugar
2 teaspoons cinnamon
3/4 cup butter or margarine, melted
8 cups apples, peeled and sliced
1/4 cup milk

Cut butter into flour and salt with a pastry cutter. Combine water and egg; add to flour. Mix. Turn out on a lightly floured board and knead 5 minutes. Divide dough into fourths. Cover with a warmed bowl and let stand 30 minutes. Combine sugar and cinnamon. Roll out dough, one part at a time, into rectangular shape. Brush

continued

Apple Strudel continued

with melted butter. Place 2 cups apple slices down one half of rectangle. Sprinkle with 1/4 of the cinnamon and sugar mixture. Fold other half of dough over and roll as for a jelly roll. Seal edges. Place roll in a crescent or straight on a greased pan. Brush top with milk and sprinkle with sugar. Repeat with rest of dough and filling. Bake in preheated 325° oven for about 60 minutes. Serve with whipped cream.

Variation 1: This makes two or three smaller strudels.

2-1/2 cups flour
1 cup butter
Pinch of salt
1/2 cup sour cream, room temperature
3 large egg yolks, room temperature
1 cake fresh yeast

Walnut filling:
1/2 pound ground walnuts
4 beaten egg whites
1-1/2 cups sugar
1 teaspoon vanilla
Dash of salt

Cut flour, butter, and salt together; set aside. In a separate bowl mix sour cream and egg yolks; dissolve yeast in mixture. Mix all ingredients together and knead until smooth. Brush dough with butter and chill overnight. Place dough on lightly floured board, divide into two or three parts, and roll out as thin as possible. Spread dough with the walnut filling or any other of choice. Roll up tightly like a jelly roll; seal edges. Place on greased baking sheet and bake at 350° for 50 to 60 minutes.

Variation 2: Freezer Strudel

2 cups flour

1/2 cup butter

Pinch of salt

2 egg yolks

Prepare dough as others, but divide and freeze in sealed containers for later use. Allow enough time to soften before use.

Date Nut Bars

Mana Machovsky Zlatohlavek, Cedar Rapids, Iowa

4 eggs
1 cup sugar
1-1/4 cups flour
2 teaspoons baking powder

1/8 teaspoon salt
1 cup chopped dates
1 cup chopped nuts
1 teaspoon vanilla

Beat eggs until foamy. Slowly add sugar and beat until thick and lemon colored. Gradually add the flour sifted with the baking powder and salt. Add chopped dates, nuts, and vanilla and mix well. Spread batter in a greased 10 x 15-inch pan and bake at 325° for 25 to 30 minutes. Cut into bars and sprinkle with powdered sugar, if desired.

Raisin Pudding

Cindy Babroski, Oviedo, Florida

1 cup brown sugar
2 cups water
1 tablespoon butter

Batter:
1 teaspoon butter
1/2 cup sugar
1 teaspoon cinnamon

1 teaspoon nutmeg
1 heaping cup flour
1/2 cup sour milk
1 teaspoon baking soda
1/2 cup raisins
Pinch of salt
1/2 cup chopped nuts (optional)

Boil brown sugar, water, and butter. Pour into a 2-quart baking dish. Mix batter ingredients; drop by tablespoons into syrup. Cover and bake 30 minutes at 350°.

Favorite Prune Pudding

2 eggs
2 tablespoons sugar
1 cup milk
3 tablespoons butter, melted
Pinch of salt
1 cup flour

2 teaspoons baking powder
Prunes, softened, pitted, halved
Cinnamon
Sugar
Whipped cream for topping

Beat eggs; mix in sugar, milk, butter, and salt. Sift together flour and baking powder, then stir into egg mixture. Pour half of batter into a buttered baking dish; cover with prunes, and sprinkle with cinnamon and sugar. Add rest of batter and bake at 350° for 30 minutes. Top with whipped cream to serve.

Rice Pudding

Juanita Loven, Guttenberg, Iowa

1/2 cup raisins
2 tablespoons brandy (optional)
2 sticks cinnamon
4 whole cloves
4 cups milk, divided
1/2 cup raw medium-grain rice
1/2 teaspoon salt

1 cup sugar
3 large eggs, beaten
1 teaspoon vanilla
1 teaspoon lemon zest
1/8 teaspoon cardamom (optional)
1/2 cup slivered almonds (optional)

Soak raisins in brandy (or water) for 20 minutes; drain. Tie cinnamon and cloves in a small clean piece of cheesecloth. Pour 2 cups milk into a heavy saucepan. Add

continued

Rice Pudding continued

spice bag and heat over low heat. When milk comes to a boil, slowly stir in rice. Cook for 30 minutes, stirring occasionally. Remove the spice bag. Continue to cook until rice is tender (15 to 30 minutes). Preheat oven to 350°. In a separate bowl, mix remaining milk, the salt, sugar, beaten eggs, vanilla, lemon zest, and cardamom. When rice is tender, remove from heat and pour the custard mixture over the rice. Mix gently until blended. Add raisins. Pour into a large buttered baking dish. Set the dish in a pan of water containing 1 inch of hot water. Bake about 30 minutes or until pudding is set and a knife comes out clean when inserted in center. (Be careful of steam from water bath when opening oven door.) Serve warm or chilled. Sprinkle each serving with almonds if desired. Serves 6.

Bread Pudding

Juanita Loven, Guttenberg, Iowa

1/3 cup raisins
2 tablespoons brandy
6 thick slices day-old bread, crusts
   removed
2 tablespoons butter or margarine,
   softened
1/2 cup brown sugar

1/2 teaspoon cinnamon
1/4 teaspoon nutmeg
3 eggs
1/3 cup sugar
1 teaspoon vanilla
Dash of salt
2-1/2 cups milk

Preheat oven to 350°. Butter a 9 x 9-inch baking pan or dish. Soak raisins in brandy for 20 minutes. Drain; reserve brandy. Spread bread with butter; cut into cubes and

continued

Bread Pudding continued

lightly press into the pan. Sprinkle with brown sugar, cinnamon, nutmeg, and raisins. In a small bowl, mix eggs, sugar, vanilla, salt, and milk. Pour over the bread. Place baking dish in a pan with 1 inch hot water. Bake for 1 hour or until knife inserted in center comes out clean. Serve warm or cool with whipped cream. Sprinkle with reserved brandy if desired. Serves 6 to 9.

Blown-glass pickle ornament is traditionally "hidden" on a tree. Whoever finds it first, opens the first present.
 —In the collection of the museum store of the National Czech & Slovak
  Museum & Library

Raspberry Kuchen

Juanita Loven, Guttenberg, Iowa

1-1/2 cups flour, divided
1/2 teaspoon salt
1/2 cup butter or margarine
2 tablespoons evaporated skim milk*
1/2 cup sugar
3 cups raspberries, fresh or frozen

Topping:
1 cup sugar
1 tablespoon flour
2 eggs, lightly beaten
1 cup evaporated skim milk*
1 teaspoon vanilla

Preheat oven to 375°. Butter a 9 x 13-inch baking pan. In a small bowl, combine 1 cup flour and salt. Cut in butter until mixture resembles coarse crumbs. Stir in milk. Pat into baking pan. In a small bowl, combine 1/2 cup flour and sugar. Sprinkle over

continued

Raspberry Kuchen continued

the pastry. Arrange raspberries over all. Prepare the topping: Combine sugar and flour in a small bowl. Stir in eggs, milk, and vanilla. Pour over berries. Bake for 40 to 45 minutes or until lightly browned.

*You may substitute regular evaporated milk or cream.

Ceramic vase, crafted in the small Slovak village of Modra, in the tradition of some of Eastern Europe's oldest ceramists known as the Habaner. Slovak and Moravian potters adopted their centuries-old designs and firing techniques to create this valued artform. Each piece is handcrafted, handpainted, and signed as a unique expression of its creator.
—In the collection of the museum store of the National Czech & Slovak Museum & Library

Prague Whipped Cream Tarts *(Rakvicky)*

Sokol Greater Cleveland Cookbook, Centennial 1997 Issue

4 egg yolks

1 cup sifted powdered sugar

Whipped cream

Beat yolks and sugar together on medium speed until light yellow in color and the consistency of a marshmallow frosting (approximately 1/2 hour). Use a pastry tube or spoon mixture into very well-greased tart pans or small muffin tins; fill half full. Place tins on a cookie sheet and bake in 325° oven for 10 minutes, or until mixture rises to the top of tins, then lower oven temperature to 225° and bake about 35 minutes more. Cool and gently remove tarts from tins. Poke a small hole in one side and, using a pastry tube, fill with whipped cream. Tarts may be made a few days in advance, however, do not fill with cream until ready to serve.

Cottage Cheese Torte

Dolores Holoubek, Phillips (Wisconsin) Czechoslovakian Community Festival

2-1/2 cups finely crushed graham
    cracker crumbs
1 cup sugar
1/2 cup butter, melted
1 teaspoon cinnamon
Filling:
4 eggs
1 cup sugar

1/8 teaspoon salt
Juice of 1/2 lemon or 1/2 teaspoon
    vanilla
1/2 pint heavy cream
3 pounds small curd cottage cheese
1/4 cup flour
1/4 cup nuts (optional)

Mix together all ingredients for crust. Reserve 3/4 cup. Butter a 9-inch torte or

springform pan. Spread the crumb mixture on the bottom and sides of pan. Prepare filling: Beat eggs and sugar until light. Add salt and lemon juice. Stir in cream; add cottage cheese and the flour. Mix well. Pour mixture into prepared pan and cover with remaining crumb mixture. Sprinkle nuts over top if desired. Bake for 1 hour at 300° or 45 minutes at 325°.

Note: You may add crushed, well-drained pineapple and a few whole or chopped maraschino cherries.

Blown-glass pineapple ornament is a symbol of friendship and hospitality.
—In the collection of the museum store of the National Czech & Slovak Museum & Library

Icebox Dessert

Fern Kaplan Fackler, Cedar Rapids, Iowa

Fern says, "My mother made this many times for guests, and we never tired of it. It was airy in texture, but very rich. At the time she began making it, in the 1930s, she truly did cool it in an icebox, as we did not have electricity in our home."

1/2 cup sugar
3/4 cup milk
Pinch of salt
2 eggs, separated
1 teaspoon vanilla
1 package unflavored gelatin

1/3 cup cold water
1 cup whipped cream
12 graham crackers, crushed
3 tablespoons melted butter
3 tablespoons powdered sugar

Mix together the sugar, milk, salt, and slightly beaten egg yolks. Cook in top of a double boiler until slightly thickened. Add vanilla. Dissolve gelatin in 1/3 cup cold water and add to the hot mixture. Beat egg whites until stiff, then add to mixture; set aside to cool a little. Fold whipped cream into the slightly cooled mixture. Mix together graham cracker crumbs, butter, and powdered sugar. Press half of the cracker mix onto bottom of 9 x 12-inch pan. Pour dessert mixture into pan and sprinkle top with remaining cracker mixture. Chill until well set.

Glass-bead Christmas spider ornament
(See legend on page 62.)

Sweet Popcorn

Fern Kaplan Fackler, Cedar Rapids, Iowa

This is an adaptation of Fern's mother's recipe, which called for 1/2 cup heavy cream, instead of the butter and water, which Fern notes is more readily at hand. The food coloring can be added to complement the season or holiday.

3 tablespoons butter

3 tablespoons water

1 cup sugar

Food coloring (optional)

4 quarts popped corn

Bring the butter, water, and sugar to a boil; stir and boil 3 minutes. Pour over the popcorn and mix well.

Blown-glass corn ornament symbolizes prosperity and fertility.

Czech Yeast Dumplings with Fruit

It is a rare traditional Czech meal that does not include some sort of dumpling. This one is the Czech version of an old Jewish favorite.

1 package dry yeast

1/2 cup warm water, divided, or 1/4 cup warm water and 1/4 cup milk

2 to 4 tablespoons sugar, divided

3 large egg yolks or 2 large whole eggs

1/2 teaspoon table salt or 1 teaspoon kosher salt

1/2 teaspoon vanilla extract (optional)

1 teaspoon lemon zest (optional)

2 cups unbleached all-purpose flour

Pitted Italian plums or apricot halves

1/2 cup butter or margarine, melted

Sugar, cinnamon-sugar, poppy seeds for sprinkling (optional)

Dissolve the yeast in 1/4 cup of warm water. Stir in 1 teaspoon sugar and let stand until foamy, 5 to 10 minutes. Add the remaining water (or milk), sugar, eggs, salt,

continued

vanilla, and/or lemon zest. Stir in the flour 1/2 cup at a time to make a soft dough. On a lightly floured surface, knead until smooth and springy, about 5 minutes. Place in an oiled bowl, turning to coat. Cover and let rise until doubled, about 1 hour. Punch down dough; fold over and press down several times. Roll the dough into a 16 x 12-inch rectangle and 1/2 inch thick and cut into 4-inch squares. Place a pitted plum or apricot half in the center of each square. (If desired insert a little sugar and/or cinnamon in the fruit.) Press the edges of dough together to enclose the fruit, form into balls, cover, and let stand until puffy, about 15 minutes. Have ready 3 quarts of boiling salted water. Carefully lower batches of the dumplings into the boiling water; cover and boil until dough is spongy, about 15 minutes. Remove with a slotted spoon and drain. Drizzle with the melted butter and topping of choice.
Note: Savor gently. Tradition says a knife spoils the flavor of the dumpling!

Contents

Cookies & More Treats

Statue on the Bridge of Lions
Czech Village, Cedar Rapids, Iowa

BOOKS BY MAIL Penfield Stocking Stuffers: You may mix titles. Postpaid: One book for $12; 2 for $20; 3 for $28; 4 for $35; 6 for $50; 12 for $90. Complete catalog of all titles $2.50. *(Prices and availability subject to change.)* Please call 1-800-728-9998.

Æbleskiver and More (Danish)
Dandy Dutch Recipes
Dutch Style Recipes
Dear Danish Recipes
Fine Finnish Foods
French Recipes
German Style Recipes
Great German Recipes
Norwegian Recipes
Norwegian Centennial
Scandinavian Holiday Recipes
Scandinavian Smorgasbord Recipes
Scandinavian Style Fish and Seafood Recipes
Scandinavian Sweet Treats
Splendid Swedish Recipes
Time-Honored Norwegian Recipes
Waffles, Flapjacks, Pancakes
Slavic Specialties

Pleasing Polish Recipes
Cherished Czech Recipes
Czech & Slovak Kolaches & Sweet Treats
Quality Czech Mushroom Recipes
Quality Dumpling Recipes
Amish Mennonite Recipes & Traditions
American Gothic Cookbook
Recipes from Ireland
Recipes from Old Mexico
Savory Scottish Recipes
Ukrainian Recipes
Tales from Texas Tables
Texas Cookoff
License to Cook Series:
Italian Style; Texas Style; Alaska Style;
Arizona Style; Iowa Style; Minnesota Style;
New Mexico Style; Oregon Style;
Wisconsin Style; Missouri Style

19th Century Immigrant Home
National Czech & Slovak Museum & Library, Cedar Rapids, Iowa